THE

BASIC INGREDIENTS

for

SPIRITUAL GROWTH

THE

BASIC INGREDIENTS

for

SPIRITUAL GROWTH

LEROY EIMS

A DIVISION OF SCRIPTURE PRESS PUBLICATIONS INC.
USA CANADA ENGLAND

Scripture quotations are from the *New King James Version.* © 1979, 1980, 1982, Thomas Nelson Publishers, and the *Amplified Bible* (AMP), *Old Testament* © 1962, 1964, by Zondervan Publishing House; *New Testament* © 1954, 1958 The Lockman Foundation; the *Holy Bible, New International Version*® (NIV). Copyright © 1973, 1978, 1984 by International Bible Society. Used by permission of Zondervan Publishing House. All rights reserved.

Copyediting: Carole Streeter and Barbara Williams
Cover Design: Mardelle Ayres
Cover Photo: William Koechling

Library of Congress Cataloging-in-Publication Data

Eims, LeRoy.
    The basic ingredients for spiritual growth/LeRoy Eims.
      p.   cm.
    ISBN 0-89693-074-2
    1. Christian life — 1960- 2. Spiritual life. I. Title.
BV4501.2.E318   1992
248.4 — dc20   92-14906
                                             CIP

---

1 2 3 4 5 6 7 8 9 10 Printing / Year 96 95 94 93 92

For my pastor

Dr. John Stevens

*whose sermons are a constant source
of inspiration and biblical insight*

*and whose leadership keeps the church
focused on the Person of Christ
and our Lord's mission throughout the world*

Contents

Preface

To many Christians spiritual growth is a mystery. They do all they know to do, but never seem to make much progress. They don't experience one year's growth in a year. The years come and go, and they remain basically the same. They consume lots of sermons. They consume lots of hot dogs at church parties. They work in the Sunday School; they sing in the choir; they serve on various boards, and are members of various circles. They try to witness, but not much happens; and, as they look back over their lives, they realize something is missing. They may wonder if going to a different church is the answer, and so they look in on a church down the street that has a greater emphasis on the Holy Spirit. Others look in on a church up the street that has a greater emphasis on Bible teaching—complete with overhead projector and multicolored marking pens. A few more years pass and they recognize that they are still in the same old rut.

This book tries to take the mystery out of spiritual growth. It covers what many have come to know as the basics of a healthy, Christ-centered, Spirit-controlled life.

Some may wonder why I included witnessing in a book

on spiritual growth. The reason is that we are called upon to be channels, not buckets. If there is no outlet, the pond becomes stagnant. Paul spoke of what Christ had accomplished "through" him. Paul was a channel of the grace of God to a needy world. If you have no outreach, your Christian life stagnates.

Others may wonder why I left certain things out — such as the place suffering plays in our growth in grace — or why there is no mention of many of the great doctrines of the Bible. The reason I did not go into these important matters is because much has been written on great themes, while such everyday, common matters like Bible reading, Scripture memory, and follow-up of new believers are often overlooked.

Which brings us to another potential question that may bother some. Should a book on the ingredients of spiritual growth contain a chapter on the follow-up and training of new believers? Shouldn't that be dealt with in a book on Christian service rather than spiritual growth? My answer to that question is both yes and no. Yes, reaching out to the young in the faith is certainly a vital and necessary aspect of the ministry of both laymen and clergy alike. But one powerful reason why we should include follow-up in a study of our own spiritual growth is this: True discipleship includes discipling others. When you and I come to the place where we are not only receiving help but passing on to others what we have learned, our own spiritual growth is accelerated. How often have you heard a Sunday School teacher say that he or she gets far more out of the lesson than the pupils in the class? Remember, nothing is truly yours until you can give it away.

The Apostle Paul told the Corinthians, "What I received I passed on to you" (1 Corinthians 15:3). Jesus spent three years discipling the apostles, and toward the end of His ministry commanded them to teach all nations "teaching them to obey everything I have commanded you" (Matthew 28:18-20). What they learned from Jesus, they were to share with others. But it didn't stop there. The people who were reached with the Gospel and became followers of Christ were to take what they had learned from the apostles and pass it on to others. The apostles were to teach them to observe all that Christ had commanded.

And when we undertake to pass along to others these basic ingredients of spiritual growth such as Scripture memory and the quiet time, we find that they take on a whole new luster and begin to sparkle and shine in our own lives like never before. Just as with witnessing, if there is no outreach, our Christian life stagnates.

It is my prayer that God will use this book to make the mysterious ingredients of spiritual growth clear and plain and set you on a path you can follow for a lifetime.

Over the past forty years, I have had the privilege of co-laboring in conferences, seminars, church camps, and weekend retreats with hundreds of men of God. Much of what appears in this book I learned from them as we shared the Word of God together. I want to acknowledge a few of these men.

Roc Bottomly	George Davis	Rollin Delap
Tommy Gowan	Ron Oertli	Harvey Soderholm
Wayne Wright	Bob Seifert	Gene Powell
Larry Blake	Don Rosenberger	Dave Medders
Dave Bertch	Lonnie Hayter	Carl Vargo
Dan Greene	Bill Tell	Danny Souder
Miles Seaborn	Richard Gregory	George Worrell

LeRoy Eims
Colorado Springs, Colorado
1992

Chapter 1

QUIET TIME

I suppose the vote would be unanimous. If you
were to go to the members of your church and ask them if
the practice of spending time alone with God was a good
idea, everyone would be for it. Some might even back up
their reasons with a passage from the Bible. Daily time
alone with God is a practice everyone applauds. But for
many, that's where it ends. Applause? Yes! Action? No!

I was first made aware of this discrepancy when I
heard Dawson Trotman tell about his interview with a
group of missionary candidates who were heading for the
mission field. Daws was a member of the board of directors
of the organization, and the leadership of the mission had
invited him to talk to the prospective missionaries to determine if they were ready for such a momentous undertaking.

Daws had one question for the candidates: "Are you
currently meeting with the Lord on a daily basis in a devotional time of prayer and Bible reading?" In simple terms,
"Do you have a quiet time?" Not one of them said yes. And
the thing that was such a shocker was the fact that these
men and women were not just your average people in the
pew. These were among the best the church had produced.

They were willing to leave loved ones and homeland for the sake of Christ.

Why do you suppose this simple practice is not taken more seriously? It seems to me that many people have never understood the benefits to their walk with the Lord. A person who goes to work for a corporation wants to know the starting salary and the long-term benefits. I think we need to look at a few of the long-term benefits the Lord brings our way as we form the practice of a daily quiet time.

Quiet Time Eases Pressures

God can use your quiet time to ease the pressures and problems of your life. I have talked to people who bring the pressures of work home with them, and then take the problems of home back to work. When these pressures become too great, an explosion can occur. I know that is true because it almost happened to me years ago when my wife and I were facing a very difficult problem in our family. We both had very heavy hearts, and we shed buckets of tears. During the time when the problem was at its worst, I was invited to go to Denver to spend a couple of days with the directors of six Christian organizations. Each of these directors brought an assistant with him and that's why I was there. After one of the meetings, Bill Bright suggested to me that we have some time of prayer together. We went to Bill's room, and he told me his organization was facing some rather stiff problems. "But," he said, "I am not under the burden of these things because I have appropriated the truth revealed in 1 Peter 5:7, 'Casting all your care upon Him for He cares for you.' The problems are still there, but the burden is lifted. I have cast them on the Lord." And then he made this amazing statement. "I have learned that either I carry them or Jesus does, but we both can't do it. And so I have cast them on Him." And there I sat with my burdened heart. After our time together, I went to my room and began to talk to God. I had memorized 1 Peter 5:7 years ago, but I had never done what Bill was talking about. So I knelt at the foot of the bed and said something like this, "Lord, I don't know if this will work or not, but right now I cast my burden on You and ask You to carry it for me. What happened next is hard to explain. I felt the burden melt away. I felt light, almost giddy. The burden was lifted, my heavy heart was healed, and I was free. The problem was still there, but the burden was gone. David explained it this way: "Cast your burden on the Lord, and He shall sustain you" (Psalm 55:22).

Many thousands of Christians have discovered the blessings that God showers down upon His people as we meet with Him day by day, reflect on His Word, claim the promises He makes, face the rigors of discipleship, unburden our hearts in prayer, offer the sacrifice of praise, and in everything give thanks. So let me ask you — are you right now facing more than your share of the pressures and problems of life? Let me encourage you to begin the lovely practice of meeting the Lord on a day-by-day basis. As you experience His transforming power and are guided by His infinite wisdom, your life will change. As you stay close to Him, He will see you through.

This great truth was brought forcibly to my mind by an incident that happened to me at O'Hare Airport in Chicago. Our plane was late getting in and I only had a few minutes to catch the connecting flight to Toronto. When I checked the monitor to see where I was supposed to go, my worst fears were realized. The plane was departing from the gate that was farthest away. And to make matters worse, the airport was so crowded I could barely move. O'Hare is always very busy, but I had never seen anything like this. I tried to hurry but was trapped in a slow-moving mob. I twisted and turned and squirmed but got nowhere fast. I was doomed to miss my flight and spend several hours waiting for the next flight. And on top of all that, I would not arrive in time to speak at my meeting. At the height of my frustration, I saw a uniformed airline employee watching me. After some time he called over to me and asked, "What's your problem?" "I'm trying to catch my plane to Toronto," I replied. "Don't worry, you'll make it," he said. "I don't see how I can possibly get to the gate on time in this crowd," I answered. He edged his way over to me and said, "If you will stay close to me, everything will be okay." "Why is that?" I asked. "Because," he replied. "I'm the pilot on that flight and they aren't going to leave without me." I almost fainted with surprise. Later a passage of Scripture came to mind, "I saw the Lord constantly before me. Because He is close by my side I will not be shaken or cast down" (Acts 2:25). What the pilot said to me suggests a great spiritual truth. In essence God says, "If you will stay close to Me, everything will be okay." David put it this way. "In Your presence is fullness of joy; at Your right hand are pleasures forever more" (Psalm 16:11).

Quiet Time Kindles Devotion

God can use our daily quiet time to fan the flame of devotion to Christ and fervency in His service. We all find our spirits growing cold from time to time. When I find this happening to me, I set aside a day to spend alone with God just to thaw out. If I leave the refrigerator door open long enough, the ice will melt. And if I leave my heart open to the Lord Jesus Christ, the spiritual ice will melt and my lost zeal will be rekindled.

Do you recall the story of Jesus cleansing the temple? He found some things going on in His house of prayer that

He didn't like, so He threw the rascals out. And as the disciples watched they were reminded of an Old Testament Scripture, "Zeal for Your house has eaten Me up" (John 2:17). Jesus Christ was consumed with a fiery zeal that left no room for a cold heart and icy spirit. This fire that burned was no temporary thing, and it had a profound effect on those around Him.

Toward the end of His time on earth, Jesus took a little walk with two disciples who were anything but on fire. In fact, the record indicates they were downhearted, confused, frightened, and their hopes were dashed. But during that walk with Jesus, an amazing transformation occurred, and they later said to each other, "Did not our heart burn within us while He talked with us on the road and while He opened up the Scriptures to us?" (Luke 24:32) After a time of communion with Jesus, their hearts began to burn. Why? As they talked, the fire spread from His heart to theirs.

If you desire a heart filled with devotion for Christ and zeal for the work of Christ, form the practice of spending some time each day in close communion with Him, and let His fire set your heart aflame. How would you like the following words to be the testimony of your life? "And in every work that he began in the service of the house of God, in the law and in the commandment, to seek his God, he did it with all his heart. So he prospered" (2 Chronicles 31:21). Those words can reflect your life if you will invest some time each day in fellowship with the Lord. He will enable you to be "fervent in spirit, serving the Lord" (Romans 12:11).

A Quiet Time Can Help Prevent Burnout

The quiet time is a great help in preventing burnout. If you go and go and go and never stop, you are going to run into problems. Some months ago I ran out of gasoline on the way to work. The car sputtered and coughed and came to a standstill. There was nothing wrong with the engine or transmission or electrical system, but there the car sat. I called a friend who went to the filling station and got a can of gas for me. And so it is in our Christian life—we must allow time to fill the tank. And that's one of the great benefits of the quiet time. It provides a means whereby we can stop and "fill up our souls" as we spend some quiet moments with God. And if we don't, we will cause trouble for ourselves and for others around us.

Now let me ask you a question. What causes burnout? Is it a result of too much hard work? My mother used to say, "LeRoy, hard work never hurt anybody." Was she wrong? No, I don't think she was. I don't think it is the work that causes us to burn out. It seems to me it happens something like this. I have lots to do so I spend lots of time doing it. And if the work piles up, I begin to look around to find some extra hours in the day. I've got to find something I can cut out to give me more time to do what I have to do. And all too often, the thing I cut out of my schedule for the really important stuff is my quiet time. And with that spiritual dimension gone, I find myself not conducting my life in the energy of the Spirit but in the energy of the flesh. And if I work long and hard in the energy of the flesh, it will soon catch up to me and I will find myself stalled along the side of the road in need of someone to come to my rescue.

Let me ask you a question? Did Jesus work long and hard hours? Of course, He did, but many do not realize that fact. Their idea of a typical day for the Lord Jesus was spending the day taking leisurely strolls through the meadows, enjoying the birds and the flowers, without a care in the world. But, the facts present quite a different picture. His life was filled with long, busy days, with death threats, with the sorrow of seeing His beloved city of Jerusalem turn its back on Him, and the pressures of fame and popularity. Notice Luke 5:15-16, "Then the report went around concerning Him all the more; great multitudes came together to hear, and to be healed by Him of their infirmities. So He Himself often withdrew into the wilderness and prayed." By His example He has taught us how to choose the priority in the midst of secondary things that demand our attention.

Look at the lesson recorded in Mark 1. Jesus was in the house of Simon and Andrew where He healed Peter's mother-in-law. And then, at evening after the sun went down, the entire city gathered outside the house in hope of finding help, and Jesus responded to their need. Now think with me for a moment. If He did not begin this ministry until after the sun went down, and He ministered to the needs of an entire city, what time do you think He went to bed? I'm sure it was in the wee hours of the morning. But nevertheless, "In the morning, having risen a long while before daylight, He went out and departed to a solitary place; and there He prayed" (v. 35). I believe the Holy Spirit led Mark to record this incident to show us the kind of priority that Jesus placed on the quiet time. Some of you may be thinking, "LeRoy, what you seem to be doing is trying to place us under some sort of legalistic bondage." Not at all. What we must see is that if we go day after day without setting aside some time for prayer and reflection on the Word, we are simply making a declaration of independence and saying to God, "I don't need the strength and grace that comes from spending time with You. I can go it alone." And that's where burnout rears its ugly head.

Having a daily quiet time is a clear declaration of our dependence on God and our commitment to live by His strength and not our own. The Prophet Isaiah speaks directly to this truth.

Have you not known? Have you not heard? The everlasting God, the Lord, the Creator of the ends of the earth, neither faints nor is weary. There is no searching of His understanding. He giveth power to the weak, and to those who have no might He increases strength. Even the youths shall faint and be weary, and the young men shall utterly fall, but those who wait on the Lord shall renew their strength; they shall mount up with wings like eagles, they shall run and not be weary, they shall walk and not faint (Isaiah 40:28-31).

From Failure to Success

Thus far in this chapter we have looked at three benefits that are ours in having a quiet time. God can use this quiet time with Him to ease the pressures and problems of life. God can use our daily quiet time to fan the flame of devotion to Christ and fervency in His service. God can use the quiet time with Him to keep us going and prevent burnout. Now let's look at two people who were totally defeated in their efforts to have a regular daily time with the Lord.

Bob's problem was his busyness. He had a small animal hospital in Sioux City, Iowa and it ran him ragged. In addition to his work at the hospital, he drove all over the place taking care of the cattle, hogs, sheep, and horses on the surrounding farms. Bob Taussig was one busy man. And whenever I talked to him about the quiet time, he told me how busy he was. I knew Bob was an Eisenhower booster, and so one day I asked him what he would do if he ever got a call from Ike asking if he would like to have an early morning breakfast with him. Well, of course, Bob said he would be honored and would make certain he had the time. It was there I reminded Bob that someone far more important than General Eisenhower wanted to meet with him on a regular basis. Bob saw it in an instant, and as far as I know, he hasn't missed a quiet time in the past thirty-five years. For Bob it was simply a matter of making an appointment.

Let me ask you a question. Is busyness keeping you from daily time with God? Make an appointment with Him in the same way you make an appointment to see the doctor. Unlike the doctor, God will not keep you waiting; He will be ready when you are. After all, it is God's idea that the two of you get together around His Word and at the throne of His grace.

The second person who struggled for years to be consistent in her daily time with God was my wife, Virginia. At night she would putter around the house finding one more thing that needed attention before she went to bed. It nearly took an act of Congress to get her to go to bed at night, and it almost took another act of Congress to get her out of bed in the morning. Her time with the Lord was practically nonexistent. After many years of defeat in this struggle, she was led to make a very simple prayer that totally revolutionized her life. She prayed that God would give her a hunger for Himself, and through a series of circumstances, that prayer was answered. Today her quiet time is a thing of beauty. She spends at least two hours each morning reading her Bible and some favorite devotional books, and spending time on her knees in prayer.

Exodus 34:2-3 gives us a simple and brief pattern to follow. "Be ready in the morning, and come up in the morning to Mount Sinai, and present yourself to Me there on the top of the mountain. And no man shall come up with you, and let no man be seen throughout all the mountain; let neither the flocks nor herds feed before that mountain."

● Be ready. For me that means making sure that the night before I put my Bible and reading glasses on my desk for me to use in the morning, so I don't waste time hunting them down when I get up.

● Present yourself to God. Many years ago I was told, "Remember, LeRoy, you are not meeting a habit. You are meeting God."

● Go to a place where you can be alone with the Lord to pray and read His Word. If the Lord lays it on your heart to start the day with Him, there is a vital truth for you in Genesis 19:27, "And Abraham went early in the morning to the place where he stood before the Lord." It is a helpful practice to go to bed at a decent hour if you want to get up early. May God grant you His joy as you meet with Him.

Chapter 2

PRAYER

I'm so glad our God is not like the weatherman we had when we lived in Lincoln, Nebraska. Every evening around 5:15, he would be on TV talking about the weather. He wouldn't come right out and tell us if it was going to rain. He would say there was a 30 percent chance of showers or 40 or 50 percent, but never a clear declaration as to whether we were going to have a storm. In the summertime, he would warn us of a 30 or 40 or 50 percent chance of a tornado coming through town the next day. In the winter, he would be equally vague about a blizzard.

Think with me for a moment. What if Jeremiah 33:3, which reads, "Call to Me, and I will answer you, and show you great and mighty things, which you do not know" read this way, "Call to Me, and there is a 30 percent chance that I will answer you"? Or what if John 16:24, which reads, "Until now you have asked nothing in My name. Ask, and you will receive, that your joy may be full," read this way, "Until now you have asked nothing in My name. Ask, and there is a good possibility that you may receive, so that your joy may be full"? How we thank the Lord that the Bible is not filled with such uncertainties. Instead, we find clear promises as to what God will and will not do. And this is clearly true in the passages of Scripture that teach us about prayer.

Let me illustrate this further. What would you do if you got on an airplane and just as you were getting settled in your seat, the captain's voice came over the intercom and said, "Ladies and gentlemen, we apologize for the delay. As you can see, our cabin personnel are going up and down the aisle to make sure we have an accurate count of just how many people we have on board. It is extremely critical today that we do not overload the airplane. Our problem is that the main runway is closed for repair, and we are forced to use a much shorter runway. Now frankly, folks, we're not sure we can make it off the ground on that short runway. We think we can. In fact, we're pretty sure we can. But we can't guarantee we will make it. So if you don't want to take the chance, this would be a good time to get off the airplane." Now, what would you do? Stay on the airplane even though there was a 30 or 40 or 50 percent chance it would not get off the ground?

How we thank the Lord He does not deal with us on those terms. Contrast the words of Jesus, "If you ask anything in My name, I will do it" (John 14:14) with something like, "Go ahead and pray; ask anything in My name, but let Me caution you not to get your hopes up. I probably won't pay any attention to what you say anyway." It seems to me that one of the great motivations to pray is the certainty that God hears us and promises to answer.

Prayer Takes Time

There are some clear instructions in the Word as to how we should approach God in prayer. Remember, God is not like a busy chief executive officer of some large corporation who sits behind his huge desk and watches as we come flying through the door to drop memos in His in-basket. We rush into His office with memos on which we have hastily scribbled our requests, toss them into His in-basket, and then turn and rush out of His presence. No, God invites us to have unhurried, meaningful fellowship with Him in prayer on a day-by-day basis. He has not accommodated Himself to the computer age. The little phrase "Time with God" still contains the word *Time.*

If we are going to have a meaningful prayer life, we must acknowledge the fact that it is going to take some time. And God is perfectly willing to let our prayer life grow and mature. We cannot build a strong prayer life on a weak foundation. I recall the night my wife learned that lesson. We were in Minneapolis attending Northwestern College. We had known the Lord only for a few months. One of the highlights of our day was when Dr. Harry Stam would come on KTIS, the school's radio station, and pray. He would tell about some missionary activity and then pray for the people involved.

When he prayed it was like being in the presence of Jesus Himself. Dr. Stam lifted us to the throne of Grace when he poured out his heart. From time to time we would have chapel speakers who would remind us that if we aspired to become men and women of God, we must learn to pray. And often they would quote people like Martin Luther and Charles Spurgeon and F.B. Meyer who spoke of spending hours in prayer.

My wife became convinced that that was what she had to do if she was going to become a truly spiritual woman. So one evening she determined to pray all night. She laid out some clean diapers just in case the baby needed attention. I promised I would listen for him and take care of any need he might have. She went out back to the screened porch, knelt down, and began her prayer vigil. She poured out her heart about everything she could think of. And then she

25

looked at her watch to see how long she had been in prayer. She assumed she had prayed for at least an hour. Was she in for a surprise! She had been in prayer for a total of two minutes. She came back in the house and went to bed, feeling defeated. But how different things are today. Every day she spends a couple of hours in the presence of God. She does not treat God like a busy executive in some huge corporation and drop memos into His in-box as she rushes in and out of the room.

Prayer Shows Us God's Character

One of the most interesting things about prayer is that it reveals in such simple and clear ways something of the character of God. Some years ago, friends of ours came to our home for a Thanksgiving dinner. Their little boy was around seven years old and he was a natural born explorer. He no sooner had his coat off than he began to investigate the house. He went from room to room and shortly came running up the stairs from the basement and asked, "What's that big green table?"

"That's a Ping-Pong table," I replied.

"What do you do with it?" he wanted to know.

"You play Ping-Pong on it," I told him.

He became all excited. "Show me! Show me!"

"Okay," I said. "Let's go." So we went downstairs and I began to tell him about the game. "We play with this little plastic ball," I told him.

"Why can't we use this fuzzy ball," he wanted to know. The fuzzy ball was a tennis ball that was laying over in the corner.

"Oh," I replied, "the fuzzy ball doesn't bounce as well as the little plastic ball." Then I called his attention to the Ping-Pong paddle and said, "We hit the ball with this paddle."

"Why don't we just toss the ball?" he wanted to know.

"Because," I replied, "the rules of the game require that we hit the ball over the net with a paddle."

"What's a net?" he wanted to know. So I showed him the net and explained the ball had to be hit over the net and land on the other side.

"Why does it have to land on the other side?" he asked.

"Because if the ball goes over the net and doesn't land on the other side, you lose the point," I explained.

"What's a point?" he asked.

"A point is what you get if you hit the ball over the net, it lands on the other side of the table, and the other person doesn't get it back to your side of the table."

"What is that white line in the middle of the table?" he inquired.

"That's used if you are playing doubles," I replied.

"What's doubles?" he asked.

Now folks, about that time I was ready to cry out, "Enough already! This kid is going to drive me nuts." And then it hit me. How different I am from God! Think of it. Here is this awesome God with all these important things that demand His attention going on all over the world, and yet He invites every one of His children to call on Him, and He hears and answers the cry of their hearts. "Go ahead," He says, "ask Me something. I will hear and answer you." And this is true even if our prayers point out our immaturity and foolishness. His patience and compassion shine through. He never cries out, "Enough already!"

Prayer Is a Matter of Life and Death

One of the most fascinating passages of Scripture on the subject of prayer was penned by the Apostle Paul in his letter to the Thessalonians, where he said, "Pray without ceasing" (5:17). When we read a verse like that we are tempted to ask, "Is this in touch with reality? Or is it just a little religious platitude that looks nice on a wooden plaque on the paneled wall of your study?" No, this verse contains words that are very much in touch with the realities of the Christian life. Obedience to this verse is a matter of life and death.

For many years my wife and I have been great fans of the *National Geographic* magazine. The pictures are beautiful and the articles are interesting. It's fascinating for us to read about people whose lifestyle is completely different from what we are used to. One of the subjects we've found fascinating is the underwater exploration that is taking place all over the world. I suppose the interest in what goes on under the sea got its start with the famous French underwater explorer, Jacques Cousteau. The sophisticated equipment they use today boggles the mind. I can recall many years ago when the only means of going to the bottom of the sea was a diving suit. The person would put on this heavy canvas suit complete with weighted shoes, a heavy headpiece with a window to look out, a long rope that he could yank if something went wrong and, most important of all, an air hose that supplied oxygen. When the diver was all set, he would jump off the side of the ship, sink to the bottom, and walk around looking for exotic fish, strange ocean plants, or treasure, all depending on his mission. Everything about the environment into which the diver went was hostile. There were a thousand things that could go wrong and cost the diver his life. For that reason, the crew above water was constantly checking the air hose connection to make sure everything was intact.

Christian, that's a fairly accurate picture of your situation every day. The environment in which you live is hostile to your spiritual growth and development. The world is always trying to squeeze you into its mold. The devil is constantly trying to lure you off the straight and narrow path, and the inner corruptions of your own flesh are constantly trying to sap your spiritual vigor. It is a life-and-death matter to keep your connections intact with your support system up above. And one of your primary needs is a strong prayer connection by which you can keep in constant touch with God and receive life-giving power and wisdom from Him. To try to go it alone is madness.

The command to pray without ceasing is not just a nice little religious platitude. It is a matter of survival. The Christian who does not keep his prayer lifeline open at all times runs the danger of spiritual disaster. Therefore, "Pray without ceasing."

Prayer Reveals the Reality of God

One of the hidden values of prayer is seen in the area of evangelism. Some months ago I was asked to present the claims of Christ to the members of a large fraternity on the campus of Ohio State University. I spoke for about thirty minutes and in closing told the men if they had any questions they should feel free to talk to me later. When the meeting broke up, a young man came to me and said, "Can you prove to me there is a God?" "Oh," I said, "I don't know if I can or not, but have a seat and I'll try." I think he expected me to get into a scientific discussion with him. I said, "One of the clearest proofs to me that there is a God is the fact that He answers my prayers." He seemed a bit surprised and said, "Tell me about that." So for the next thirty minutes or so, I shared with him some of the answers to prayer that I have received over the years. The Lord used that time to cause the young man to open his heart to the realization that there really is a personal God who loves us and cares for us and whose Son died for us. Prayer can be a great resource in evangelism.

Roadblocks to Prayer

On a number of occasions the Apostle Paul used illustrations from a variety of sports such as track and field, boxing and wrestling, to illustrate various aspects of the Christian life. Let's look at two of our most popular sports today to gain insights into a vital aspect of prayer.

Some time ago I was watching a football game. The quarterback took a few steps back, looked down the field, and threw a pass to one of his teammates. The man caught the pass and headed for the goal line. As he was running at breakneck speed, he looked up and saw two huge men intent on stopping him. They did, and he didn't make it to the goal.

The same thing happened in a championship basketball game. A nimble-fingered young man reached out and plucked the ball from the hands of a player on the opposing team and headed down the court. As he approached the basket, he looked up and there stood a six-foot eight-inch gentleman from the other team with his arms up in the air. The man tried to shoot the ball into the basket, but his shot was blocked and fell short of the basket.

As you and I reflect on those things that contribute to our spiritual growth, it becomes evident to us that there are some things that can block our effectiveness in prayer. Let's look at a few of these roadblocks that are revealed to us in the Bible.

● The first is located in Psalm 66:18: "If I regard iniquity in my heart, the Lord will not hear." Unconfessed sin blocks our forward progress in prayer. If I am playing with sin, my prayers will go unheard and unanswered.

• A second hindrance is unbelief. It is an affront to God to go to Him in prayer and lay out our requests, while in the back of our minds we are saying, "Here are my requests, but I don't think You are willing or able to answer them." If we have that attitude we might as well save our breath to cool our soup. James tells us to go to the Lord in prayer, but he says that we must "ask in faith, with no doubting, for he who doubts is like a wave of the sea driven and tossed by the wind. For let not that man suppose that he will receive anything from the Lord" (James 1:6-7). Also note carefully Isaiah 59:1-2, "Behold, the Lord's hand is not shortened, that it cannot save; nor His ear heavy, that it cannot hear. But your iniquities have separated you from your God; and your sins have hidden His face from you, so that He will not hear."

• Third, Jesus ties our intake of the Word of God to the assurance of answered prayer. He said, "If you abide in Me, and My words abide in you, you will ask what you desire, and it shall be done for you" (John 15:7).

• Fourth, our prayers will be hindered if we refuse to obey when God speaks to us. In Proverbs 28:9, we read, "One who turns away his ear from hearing the law, even his prayer shall be abomination." If we do not give heed when God speaks, we will not be heard by God when we pray. Recently I read these words from John R. Mott.

For many years it has been my practice in traveling among the nations of the world to make a study of the sources of the spiritual movements which are doing most to vitalize and transform individuals and communities. At times it has been difficult to uncover the hidden spring, but invariably where I have had the time and patience to do so, I have found it in an intercessory prayer life of great reality.

Recently I came across the following evaluation of prayer, "It is easy to see the importance of prayer by the prominence given it in the Bible and the prominence given it by people who have been used of God in a mighty way."

I close this chapter with a few basic tips about prayer that will aid you in your spiritual growth.

- Pray in faith (Matthew 21:22).

- Pray in Jesus' name (John 16:24).

- Pray in accordance with God's will (1 John 5:14-15).

- Remember how prayer and obedience are bonded together (1 John 3:22).

May the cry of our hearts be, "Lord, teach us to pray."

Chapter 3

BIBLE READING

Bible reading can easily get lost in the shuffle. I've found this true in my own life. But when I'm in a Bible study group, I know it's important to have my studying done by the time the group meets. Peer pressure keeps me plugging away on my study week after week. Scripture memory is usually included in the activities of our study group, and so I find that I work on my Scripture verses rather diligently. Going to church where I can hear the Word is a built-in part of my week. But not Bible reading.

No one is going to ask me what portions of Scripture I read that week. And so, with a busy schedule and lots of demands on my time, my Bible reading can get lost in the shuffle. But that need not happen. And one of the greatest preventatives against defeat in regular Bible reading is to realize the importance that God places on it. God is very clear in His desire that His people read the Bible every day. Just look at the instructions He gave to the ruler of Israel:

It shall be, when he sits on the throne of his kingdom, that he shall write for himself a copy of this law in a book, from the one before the priests, the Levites. And it shall be with him, and he shall read it all the days of his life, that he may learn to fear the Lord his God and be careful to observe all the words of this law and these statutes, that his heart may not be lifted above his brethren, that he may not turn aside from the commandment to the right hand or to the left and that he may prolong his days in his Kingdom, he and his children in the midst of Israel (Deuteronomy 17:18-20.

Could anything be clearer than that? God was so keenly interested in the King being able to read the Bible daily that he had him write out a copy for himself from the scrolls in the custody of the priests of the sanctuary. I'm sure the King had his hands full of the affairs of the nation. But God was telling him to put first things first. Bible reading was to take top priority over other things that were pressing. And how long was this to go on? All the days of his life! And to what purpose? So that he might be able to discuss the weighty matters of the Law? So that he might become a more interesting conversationalist? No. The purpose in reading the Bible was that he might gain a greater reverence for the Lord his God and live a life of obedience to His Word. Constant exposure to the Word would create in him a humble spirit that God could use to keep him from the deadly sin of pride.

A New Testament counterpart is found in James.

But be doers of the Word, and not hearers only, deceiving yourselves. For if any one be a hearer of the Word and not a doer, he is like a man observing his natural face in a mirror; for he observes himself, and goes away, and immediately forgets what kind of man he was. But he who looks into the perfect law of liberty and continues in it, and is not a forgetful hearer but a doer of the Word, this one will be blessed in what he does (James 1:22-25).

God's Inexhaustible Resource

But you might be asking, "What's so remarkable about *that* Book? Why the constant harangue about reading the Bible?" Many years ago I heard Dawson Trotman give an answer to that question. He suggested that we go outside and walk along the path and look at the soil. Why the soil? There are lots of things more spectacular than dirt. But take a moment to reflect on what comes out of the ground. You probably have a cotton shirt or blouse in your closet. Where did the cotton plant come from? From out of the ground.

Quite possibly you own a wool suit. Where did the wool come from? From sheep, who ate the grass growing out of the ground, from that nourishment grew the wool that eventually became your suit. Where did the automobile companies get the metal to make your car? They dug it out of the ground. Where did the gasoline companies get the gas and oil to run your car? From out of the ground.

Where did the gold come from that you now wear on your finger as a ring? From out of the ground. Where did the diamond come from by which you announced your engagement? From a diamond mine deep in the ground. How about the vegetables you eat at mealtime? They came from out of the ground. You build a fire—where does the coal or wood come from? From out of the ground. How about the paper for this book you are reading? It came from out of the ground. Isn't it just like the Lord to take something so plain as the soil of the earth, and bring forth so many wonderful things from it.

Now we all know what we have just read is a poor comparison to the Bible. But if we were to take the time and space, we could dwell at great length on the benefits we receive from the Bible. In this wonderful Book we receive light to keep us on the right path. It is a lamp unto our feet. It is spiritual food—our milk and meat to nourish our souls.

It is our sword by which we move forward in our spiritual battles. The Bible is our shield of faith. And how is our faith produced? "So then faith comes by hearing, and hearing by the Word of God" (Romans 10:17). What is the seed we sow to grow a spiritual crop for the Lord? "The sower sows the Word" (Mark 4:14).

As we reflect on all this, we ask ourselves the question, "Why do we find it so difficult to maintain a regular reading program?" When we consider all that the Word of God contains, and when we reflect on the many ways that God uses His Word on our behalf, this great inexhaustible gold mine, this great silver mine, diamond mine, this vast spiritual supermarket, this shining light to aid us through the dark, this sharp two-edged sword that God has given for victorious battle with the enemy of our souls, why do we find it so difficult to avail ourselves of all this?

I think it is a satanic drive against the church, against the people of God, to keep them from reading their Bibles. The devil is aware of the power of the Word, and remembers the defeat he experienced when the Lord Jesus had it out with him and overcame his threefold temptation with His threefold "It is written." But we know that there are millions of Christians who never even crack the Book. And this surprises us when we remember all that the Word of God provides for our spiritual well-being.

All of us freely confess we need guidance, cleansing, food, a shield, and a sword. Along with that confession there needs to be a desire and commitment to set aside some time each day to read His wonderful Word all the days of our lives. And we need never fear that one day we will exhaust its treasures. Early in my Christian life I read about one of the greatest Bible scholars who ever lived, Dr. A.T. Pierson. He had read the Bible every morning for fifty years, from 5:00 until 8:00 A.M. And the year he died he told a colleague, "I am just beginning to scratch the surface."

The Bible Must Take Priority

One thing I have found helpful in Bible reading is to do what I can to eliminate distractions. Some years ago, a newspaper boy came to our house asking if we would like to take the paper. I told him no. We were home so little it really wasn't worth it to subscribe to a newspaper. He persisted. He was trying to win a contest and get a free trip to Disneyland. The newspaper was making a special offer and e could have the first month free. He continued with his sales pitch along with an occasional pitiful, "Oh please, mister, help me win a trip to Disneyland!" He assured me that if, after taking the paper free for a month, I didn't want to continue, it was perfectly okay to cancel my subscription. I finally gave in. The next morning I got out of bed, sat down in an easy chair beside the bed, and began my Bible reading. I had no sooner gotten started when I heard a kerthump against the door. It was the arrival of the newspaper. I tried to keep reading the Bible, but my mind kept wandering. I wondered what was going on in the world that morning, so I closed my Bible, went downstairs, opened the door, got the newspaper, and learned what was going on in the world. The next morning I went to my chair, opened my Bible and began to read. Kerthump! There it was again. And once again I closed my Bible, went downstairs, opened the door, picked up the newspaper, and learned what was happening in the world. The next morning I got out of bed, settled down in my chair, opened my Bible, and began to read. Kerthump. I was out of the chair like a shot, ran down the stairs, opened the door, and told the lad I couldn't take the paper anymore. He asked why. I told him I just couldn't handle it. He said, "Okay." And that ended that. I suppose some of you are saying, "LeRoy, you should have had the willpower to resist." Of course, I should. But I didn't, and therefore I had to take the necessary steps to eliminate the distraction.

Sometimes it is not a matter of eliminating distraction but of making a choice. My wife and I were in Florida speaking for a week at an International Convention of Christian Businessmen. After the evening meeting, Virginia and I went to our room and retired early. We were tired and knew we needed to get to sleep, because the schedule for the next day was going to be rather heavy. About midnight we were awakened by the arrival of the couple next door. Immediately they turned on the television and began reruns of an old cops and robbers show. Fortunately, my wife and I went back to sleep, and early the next morning we got up and began to read our Bibles. After an hour or so when we went to breakfast, we didn't hear our neighbors stirring. We went to the meeting and after it had been in progress for about thirty minutes, they came staggering into the room, still half asleep. That went on the whole week. They made the wrong choice every night. They traded old reruns of "Dragnet" or "Perry Mason" for time with the Lord.

Time with the Lord Helps Us Shine

Another good reason for consistent Bible reading is found in Philippians 2:14-15. "Do all things without murmuring and disputing, that you may become blameless and harmless, children of God, without fault in the midst of a crooked and perverse generation, among whom you shine as lights in the world."

Once when my youngest son, Randy, and I were traveling together, each evening we would read the Bible together. We had read where the Apostle Paul admonished the Philippians to "shine as lights in the world." When I asked Randy what this passage was all about, he answered, "We should be shiny." Good answer. But later on it occurred to me that being shiny is not all that easy. And that's where Bible reading comes in. You and I have no built-in light that shines in this world. Whatever shining we do must be a reflection of the light of Christ.

Years ago, when I was working as a depot agent for the Chicago Great Western Railroad, one of my primary jobs was to hand the train order to the engineer and conductor as the train roared through town. We did this by means of a forked stick where the train order was attached. The engineer and conductor would put their arm through the fork at the end of the stick and catch the order. But we had a problem. It was difficult to see the stick at night, and sometimes they would miss the order and be forced to stop the train, back up, and get their orders. Then someone had a great idea. Why not cover the forked end of the stick with paint that would glow in the dark? That way the engineer and conductor could catch the orders, and avoid having to back up the train. All the depot agent had to do was attach the orders, hold the forked stick up to the light which made it glow, and then hand it to the two officials on the train.

All went well until one night I forgot to hold the stick up to the light. I ran outside, held up the orders, and the engineer missed them. He couldn't see them because the stick was not shining. And so it is with you and me. If we fail to spend time with the Lord in daily communion with Him, it will be impossible to obey the admonition of Scripture to be a shining light in our darkened world. To reflect the light of Christ requires daily exposure to His light. And He has given us His Word as the means whereby we can spend time with Him. But if in our haste we fail to spend time in His presence, and plunge out into the day without that glow that only He can give, two things happen. Without His Word we have no lamp for our feet and light for our path; and we provide no light for others. Daily Bible reading can remedy those two problems.

The Bible's Message Is Clear

I know that some people avoid reading the Bible because they are convinced it is too difficult for them to understand. But remember this: the Bible was written to ordinary people just like you and me. And today we can buy any number of Bibles that are written in clear, plain, understandable language. The Lord went to great lengths to assure us we can understand His Word that He has given. One passage that gives that assurance is Deuteronomy 30:11-14.

> For this commandment which I command you today, it is not too mysterious for you, nor is it far off. It is not in heaven, that you should say, "Who will ascend into heaven for us and bring it to us, that we may hear it and do it?" Nor is it beyond the sea, that you should say, "Who will go over the sea for us and bring it to us, that we may hear it and do it?" But the Word is very near you, in your mouth and in your heart, that you may do it.

God did not give us His Word to confuse us. He gave us His Word that we might place our trust in Him and have a clear road map to follow in our journey with Him. We are reminded of the words of the psalmist, "I am a stranger in the earth; do not hide Your commandments from me. . . . I have chosen the way of truth; Your judgments I have laid before me" (Psalm 119:19, 30). Here he acknowledges he is a stranger who has never before traveled the path he is on. But he has a clear road map laid out before him, a road map he knows he can understand and one in which he can place his trust. That's what you and I can do day by day. In the morning, we can unfold our spiritual road map and check our course for the day.

A few years ago our family was traveling in the Midwest. We stayed overnight in a motel in Omaha and when morning came, I quietly dressed, took my Bible, and went down to the coffee shop. I was sitting at the counter sipping my coffee and reading my Bible when a man sat down beside me. He glanced my way and asked, "Is that a Bible you are reading?" "Yes," I answered. "I began the practice of starting the day with my Bible years ago." "You know," he replied, "this would be a different world if all of us did that."

And if all of us did, we would soon discover that when we have placed our faith in Christ and begun to read His Word, we would find it to be a Book we can understand. It *has* to be. Put yourself in the shoes of the people at Ephesus when their letter arrived from Paul. I'm sure there was great excitement among the people when they saw the messenger coming their way with Paul's letter to them. As he approached the crowd, there must have been great applause and shouts of joy as the people gathered to hear what Paul had to say. And then one in the congregation pointed to a long line of camels making their way to the church, each one carrying a huge load of books. "What are those books?" someone shouted. The man who had brought the letter said, "Oh, those are the commentaries you can use to help you understand Paul's letter!" Now, I am not knocking commentaries. I use them. But the thing to remember is that the Bible itself is its own best commentary. And if each of us began our day by reading His Word, we would discover two things: We *can* understand it, and the world *will* be a better place—beginning with us. As we come to the close of this chapter, some of you may be wondering how Bible reading differs from Bible study. It seems to me it is simply a matter of emphasis. Doing Bible study is like going on a search. A topical study on the subject of love might lead you to spend two or three weeks digging into the Book of 1 John, or 1 Corinthians 13, or Deuteronomy 6 and so on. Bible reading, on the other hand, is not like a search but more like a stroll in a beautiful garden. You are not looking for anything in particular. You are just moving through the Bible enjoying what you see. I had an experience during my high school days that illustrates this point. I was riding my bike downtown when suddenly there on the sidewalk was a $1 bill. I could hardly believe it. It was almost too good to be true. And that's how it is with Bible reading. You are not spending days pouring over one chapter. You are moving through the Bible three or four chapters at a time enjoying the scenery along the way.

I would like to give you four "How to's" that I have found helpful in my daily Bible reading.

- Use an accurate, clear translation.

- Read straight through the Bible in a systematic way.

- Record your discoveries either in the margin of your Bible or a notebook.

- Strive for consistency. Just as you have set times for your breakfast, lunch, and dinner, have a time for taking in your spiritual food as well.

George Müller, one of the most remarkable men of faith who ever lived, is reported to have made these remarks. "I believe that the one chief reason that I have been kept in happy useful service is that I have been a lover of Holy Scripture. It has been my habit to read the Bible through four times a year in a prayerful spirit to apply it to my heart, and to practice what I find there. I have been for sixty-nine years a happy man; happy, happy, happy."

Chapter 4

BIBLE STUDY
AND MEDITATION

Not long ago a man I'll call Charlie told me about
the many years he had lived as a Christian without any
discernible spiritual growth. He was reared in a Christian
home, and his parents were faithful in taking him to Sunday
School and church. When he was in junior high school, he
went to a youth camp where the Lord spoke to him about
the salvation of his soul. When Charlie returned home, his
parents talked to him about Christ, and in the living room of
their home, in the presence of his parents and his pastor, he
personally invited Christ to come into his heart as his Savior
and Lord. That was the beginning of his Christian life but
for the next seven years, he did not grow one inch spiritually.

When he graduated from high school Charlie enrolled
at a nearby university with three goals in mind. One, he
wanted to play college baseball; two, he wanted to get a
degree in business so that he could make lots of money; and
three, having heard that that particular university had the
best looking girls in the Southwest Conference, he wanted
to date some of those young ladies.

About the end of his sophomore year in college, he

injured his arm and was no longer able to play baseball. He was on the verge of flunking out in school because he was not studying; and the girl he was dating dumped him.

As a result of all this, he was very unhappy. When he reflected on the way his life was going, he felt sick of his lifestyle and depressed. About that time he met a young man who was a part of a Christian group on campus and they became friends. Soon Charlie's new friend began to talk to him about fellowship with God. Very simply and in an unthreatening manner, he began to share with this unhappy and depressed young man the joy that he had discovered in personal Bible study. Even though Charlie had grown up in the church, he had never really studied the Bible on his own and knew very little about it. So he determined that he would begin to study the Bible with a view to applying it to his life. He became active in a Christian group on campus and began to dig into the Word and grow spiritually.

When Charlie shared this story with me, he had been diligently studying the Bible for ten years, and had been used of God to help scores of other young men and women learn the joy of digging into the Word through personal study of the Scriptures. His excitement over Bible study reminds me of the words of the Psalmist, "I rejoice at Your Word as one that finds great treasure" (Psalm 119:162).

My problem with Charlie's story is that I've heard it over and over and over again, almost word for word. A person meets the Lord and it isn't until years later that he begins to experience spiritual growth and make genuine progress in his Christian life. And all too often the problem has a very simple solution. What the person needs to do is begin a regular intake of the Word of God through Bible study, with a view to personal application to life. And that is not a complicated, mysterious process. But most people don't study the Bible for one of two reasons: some don't know how, and others who know how aren't motivated.

Why Should We Study the Bible?

Let's take a little time to look at each of these, beginning with motivation. Why should we study the Bible? There are a number of Scriptures that speak directly to this point.

● I believe our greatest motivation for Bible study is found in the words of Jesus Himself. Referring to the Scriptures, our Lord said, "These are they which testify of Me" (John 5:39). The great desire of all Christians should be to have a growing knowledge of the Lord Jesus Christ. "For my determined purpose is that I may know Him, that I may progressively become more deeply and intimately acquainted with Him, perceiving and recognizing the wonders of His person more strongly and more clearly" (Philippians 3:10, AMP). And how do we grow in our knowledge of Christ? Through the study of the Scriptures, because the Scriptures reveal Him to our hearts.

Do you want to grow in your knowledge of Christ? If so, begin to dig into the Word through personal Bible study. About twenty years ago I was given a copy of a yearly Bible study calendar published in New Zealand. In the introduction I read these profound words, "The Bible will be found everywhere full of Christ to the patient seeker, who is ever expecting to find Him; and every history and prophecy, every type and shadow, will become a lattice through which the Beloved will reveal Himself to the soul that is waiting for Him."

● A second motivation for Bible study is found in the words of Paul to Timothy, "Be diligent to present yourself approved to God, a worker who does not need to be ashamed, rightly dividing the Word of truth" (2 Timothy 2:15). One of the burning desires of every earnest believer should be a hunger to know what pleases God and then to follow His commands with all diligence.

All too often we discover that what pleases God displeases many of those around us. Virginia and I learned this early in our Christian life. We had become Christians through reading the Bible, and there began to grow in our hearts a desire to serve the Lord. We went to our pastor and he advised us to go off to Northwestern Bible College in Minneapolis. We immediately began to make plans to head in that direction. I quit my job and we sold, gave away, or burned most of the stuff we owned, and went to Minneapolis and enrolled in school. Many people who watched all of this thought we were crazy and told us so. We were too young in the Lord to know how to explain what we were doing in such a way that people could understand. But we knew that deep in our hearts we had perfect peace and the knowledge that what we were doing pleased the Lord.

Now, after forty years of Bible study, we can look back and see the scriptural pattern that unfolded around us. We had presented ourselves to Him to do His will, and in so doing we discovered that His will was good, acceptable, and perfect. And since we were in the center of His perfect will, we had a perfect peace amid all the urgings and admonitions to do otherwise. God continues to reveal to us what pleases Him as we study the Word of truth.

• A third reason for personal Bible study can be found in Proverbs 2:1-5.

My son, if you receive my words, and treasure my commandments within you, so that you incline your ear to wisdom, and apply your heart to understanding; yes, if you cry out for discernment, and lift up your voice for understanding; if you seek her as silver, and search for her as for hidden treasures; then you will understand the fear of the Lord, and find the knowledge of God.

Here our attention is directed to the fear of the Lord which is the beginning of wisdom, and to the knowledge of God which is the ultimate wisdom. And how do we discover the wisdom of God? It is obvious that God does not reveal His ultimate wisdom to the casual, occasional seeker. No, it is revealed to those who cry out to God in prayer, who lift up their voices to Him, who search the Word of God in a study of the Scriptures as people seek for hidden treasure. The Bible is not like a frozen TV dinner that you can pop into the microwave. God's deeper revelations come after a long and diligent search.

Some time ago I learned about a treasure hunt off the coast of Florida. A group of men had become convinced that there was a fortune in Spanish gold waiting for them on the ocean floor. They knew the search would be costly and long. But they were convinced the treasure could be found and that it was worth the cost.

Christian, do you desire a deeper and greater knowledge of Christ? Do you desire a life approved by God, a life that pleases Him? Do you desire to have insight into the wisdom of God? If so, be prepared to invest in years of diligent Bible study. Are the spiritual benefits worth the spiritual effort? You *know* they are! And God is waiting for you to begin your search.

• Another tremendous benefit of Bible study is that it provides a sure, solid foundation for your faith. Paul's desire was "that we should no longer be children, infants, tossed to and fro and carried about with every wind of doctrine, by the trickery of men, in the cunning craftiness by which they lie in wait to deceive" (Ephesians 4:14). God's desire is that our faith be more solid than the Rock of Gibraltar, a faith that holds us steady like an anchor of the soul, both sure and steadfast. To help us see what that means, God points us to Abraham who "did not waver at the promise of God through unbelief, but was strengthened in faith, giving glory to God, and being fully convinced that what He had promised He was also able to perform" (Romans 4:20-21).

The summer before I enrolled in the fall term at the University of Washington in Seattle, I really bore down in Bible study. For two years I had been a student at Northwestern College and had enjoyed being immersed in a wonderful Christian atmosphere. The classes were opened and dismissed by prayer. Daily chapel service was a thrill to my heart. And now, here I was, poised on the threshold of a year at a secular campus. I studied such passages as Proverbs 3:25-26, "Be not afraid of sudden terror, nor of trouble from the wicked when it comes; for the Lord will be your confidence, and will keep your foot from being caught." Psalm 37:31 became a source of comfort and confidence, "The Law of his God is in his heart; none of his steps shall slide." God used His Word to remind me that I must put on the whole armor of God, if I was going to be victorious in the battle against the wily schemes of the devil and the rulers of the darkness of this world. Believe me, Bible study took on a whole new dimension. I knew I needed a faith that would stand the test. And it turned out that I was right. My anthropology professor taught the theory of evolution as a fact. My literature professor produced books for us to read that were saturated with such themes as greed, lust, hate. My political science professor ruled out God as a solution to anything. If there was a God, He was old and feeble and needed to be propped up by our support. It was an interesting year. And I came out of it spiritually stronger than I went in, thanks to the grace of God and the efforts of the local Navigator representative who consistently prayed for me and encouraged me to maintain a weekly Bible study. As I reflect on that year, I am reminded of the old hymn,

How firm a foundation, ye saints of the Lord,
is laid for your faith in His excellent Word.

And one primary means of developing a strong, sure, firm, bedrock faith is to maintain a consistent intake of the Word through personal Bible study.

How Should We Study the Bible?

We now turn our attention to the "how to" of Bible study. It is important that we do this, even though there are some who choke at the idea of teaching people how to study or memorize or have a quiet time. But the Apostle Paul had no such reservations. Note his comment to the Thessalonians, "We urge you, brethren, and exhort in the Lord Jesus that you should abound more and more just as you received from us *how* ye ought to walk and to please God." Notice that Paul did not admonish the Thessalonians simply to please God. He taught them *how* to do it. That's what happened to me when some friends taught me the importance of Bible study. They also showed me how to get started. I learned later they were following a little plan they had learned from Dawson Trotman, the founder of the Navigators. It was Dawson's conviction that we must tell people *what,* tell them *why,* show them *how,* get them *started,* and keep them *going.* When they introduced me to personal Bible study, they shared with me the five principles that made for a good study plan.

● First, my study was to be an original investigation. That meant it was to be a study of the Bible itself, not a study of books about the Bible. In fact, using helps like commentaries was out. I wasn't to let Matthew Henry do my work for me, but to study for myself. The Navigators had interesting little sayings they would pass along such as, "Honey eaten directly from the honeycomb has seven times the food value as does boiled or strained honey." To study the passage with the use of a commentary was to get the message after it had been strained through the thoughts of another person. I learned it was better to drink directly from the spring than to drink from the creek a mile or two downstream. In case you are wondering, I now have three sets of commentaries that I enjoy using; but I am very grateful for the training I received from men who taught me the value of original investigation—studying the Bible for itself.

• Second, Bible study should be consistent and systematic. *Consistency* carries with it the idea of doing something regularly. *Systematic* means that there should be some plan to follow that enables us to get the most out of it. I like to help people get started in a deductive study set in the framework of a simple question-and-answer study book. The Navigators Design for Discipleship books are an example of this kind of study.

They are designed to lay the groundwork for an inductive study which follows. An inductive study many people use, "Search the Scriptures" is structured around five major themes.

• What does the passage say? In answer to that question you can either summarize the chapter in your own words or outline the chapter. If you choose to write a summary it should be no longer than an average of eight words per verse. For example, if the chapter had ten verses your summary should be no longer than eighty words.

• The second question has to do with parallel passages. As you cross reference the verses in the chapter you are studying with verses from other portions of Scripture, you are shining the light of the Word of God on those verses. This is extremely helpful because the Bible is its own best commentary.

• What in this chapter don't you understand? Simply list your questions, but don't try to find the answer to each one. You will be amazed how the Holy Spirit will show you the answer in your study a few weeks later.

• What does this chapter say to you personally that you might apply to your life? In what way are you falling short? Give a specific example.

• What are you going to do about it?

I recall when I was using this plan in 1950 to study Paul's letter to the Colossians. In chapter 3 God spoke to me from verse 8 which says that I should put off anger. But I had a problem — a very quick temper. So I decided I would make application of verse 8 to my life. The Bible said I should put off anger. I was falling short of the teachings of this verse because I blew up quite easily. For instance, when I was driving downtown, there was this idiot who turned left right in front of me and almost took off my front fender. I rolled down my window, shook my fist, screamed at him, and threatened to knock his teeth out. When I got home I wrote out a rather simple plan that answered the question, "What am I going to do about my hot temper?" David must have had a personal application in mind when he wrote, "I thought about my ways, and turned my feet to Your testimonies" (Psalm 119:59). Jeremiah's words also touch on personal application, "Let us search out and examine our ways, and turn back to the Lord" (Lamentations 3:40).

On Paul's second missionary journey, he and Silas met the Bereans. We meet them in Acts 17:11, "These were more fair-minded than those in Thessalonica, in that they received the Word with all readiness, and searched the Scriptures daily to find out whether these things were so." In this passage Luke compares the Bereans with the Thessalonians. They were people who searched the Scriptures daily. Their examination of Scripture was not superficial, but was a daily practice. They were eager to invest their time and their energy to find out what the Bible said about the message Paul brought to them.

Why Should We Meditate on God's Word?

One of the outstanding benefits of careful Bible study is that it can lead to the blessed practice of meditation. Today meditation is a lost art. We are people on the go, active, busy, and in a hurry. So the idea of taking out a portion of a day to sit and do nothing but reflect is considered by many a waste of time.

However, God commands us to slow down, sit down, and think upon His Word. "Meditate on these things; give yourself entirely to them, that your progress may be evident to all" (1 Timothy 4:15).

The word *meditate* carries with it the idea of depth. It calls to mind the bass keys on the piano keyboard, a deep tone rather than a high and light one. Meditation takes discipline and time. We are more prone to "go over" lightly rather than take the time to search out the depth of meaning. We would rather pick a few loose nuggets on the hillside than dig for the treasure hidden in the earth.

● God has made some staggering promises to the man or woman who will give serious thought and attention to His Word. Consider just two of them. "This Book of the law shall not depart from your mouth, but you shall meditate in it day and night, that you may observe to do according to all that is written in it. For then you will make your way prosperous, and then you will have good success" (Joshua 1:8). God promises success to the person who will meditate on His Word.

Joshua was up to his neck in the serious business of providing leadership for the Children of Israel. This word from God came to him at a time when he was busier than he had ever been in his life, and was carrying greater responsibility than he had ever in his wildest dreams imagined. In the midst of his battle campaigns and with all the problems of leadership, the Word of God was to be central in his thinking.

"Blessed is the man who walks not in the counsel of the ungodly, nor stands in the path of sinners, nor sits in the seat of the scornful. But his delight is in the law of the Lord, and in His law he meditates day and night. He shall be like a tree planted by the rivers of water, that brings forth its fruit in its season whose leaf also shall not wither; and whatever he does shall prosper" (Psalm 1:1-3). This promise is lost to many people because it is so familiar. Children memorize it in Sunday School and Vacation Bible School, and pastors quote it from the pulpit. The words are charming and melodic, but they are also absolutely true. Let those words jar you—"Whatever he does shall prosper." Can that really be true? There's only one way to find out. Try it!

The word *meditate* carries with it the idea to revolve in the mind, to attend to carefully. And I believe that is the reason God makes those remarkable promises to the one who will do so. It indicates great esteem for what God says and shows that we hold His Word in the highest honor. God is pleased with and blesses abundantly the person who will meditate on His Word.

● Another benefit of meditation is the way it stimulates spiritual growth. Nutritionists tell us it is not so much what we eat that keeps us going, but what we assimilate. Meditation helps us assimilate the Word of God into our spiritual bloodstream and thus be "nourished in the words of faith" (1 Timothy 4:6). How do we meditate? Let's say a young man goes to Honolulu for a week's vacation. While there he receives a letter from his girlfriend who writes, "I hope you are having a good time. We certainly are. Last night we went to the game, the night before we went to a birthday party, and the night before that we attended a concert at the church." As the young man reads the letter he asks himself, "Who is *we?*" So he reads the letter again and again trying to get further light on who *we* might be. That's meditation.

Meditation differs from Bible study in that study normally requires some tools such as a study guide, a concordance, and possibly even a Bible dictionary. Meditation requires none of them. To meditate means you simply look long and hard at the passage and revolve it in your mind.

Meditation cannot be done in a hurry. In 1963 when I visited London on a preaching tour, our schedule allowed us a day of sightseeing. A young man on our university team was assigned to be our tour guide. He was eager to show us the sights and sounds of his beloved city, and arrived early in the morning armed with a list of historic places and the subway schedule. He had it all figured out, exactly when the underground railway would arrive at each point, how much time we had there, and when we had to leave to catch the train for the next stop.

I entered into this sightseeing with the sort of excitement you'd expect to find in a boy from Neola, Iowa, who is about to see the big city. David was the athletic type, in top physical shape, and he kept us on the move. We jogged through the cathedrals, sprinted through the parks, paused momentarily to gaze at the statues and cast hasty glances at buildings that oozed grandeur and history. We really saw London — but did we?

Some years later my wife and I were there on another preaching assignment, and our last day was spent with some people seeing the sights. Our pace was leisurely. I absorbed the beauty and majesty of the cathedrals I had jogged through some years before. This time my spirit was affected. I had time to really experience them, to sense their meaning and message.

God wants to communicate with us through His Word. If we take time to meditate, we will experience the depth and the greatness of the message, and the Spirit of God will speak to us and affect our lives. And here's an important point. It is God who does it, not the words printed on paper. God uses His Word as a means, as an instrument to communicate Himself to us. "My soul cleaves to the dust; revive me according to Your Word" (Psalm 119:25). Note that it was God Himself who could breathe new life into the psalmist; He used His Word as an instrument to do it.

A love for God's Word prompts meditation. The psalmist said, "Oh how I love Your Law. It is my meditation all the day" (Psalm 119:97). Christian, that's the place to start. Ask God to give you a love and delight in His Word. "And I will delight myself in Your commandments, which I love" (Psalm 119:47). Deep meaningful meditation will follow.

May God give you grace to carry out this noble practice of searching the Scriptures daily and meditating on His Word.

SCRIPTURE MEMORY

S c r i p t u r e m e m o r y rarely draws a crowd. Next to other means of Scripture intake, such as Bible study and listening to sermons, it does not win a popularity contest. Over the years the Navigators have sponsored conferences to help people in their spiritual growth. Some of these conferences have been quite large, offering a wide variety of workshops from which the conferees could make a choice.

Workshops on "How to Study the Bible," "How to Know the Will of God," "How to Witness" and "How to Have a Quiet Time" were usually well attended. But there was one that never seemed to attract very many people. In fact, there were times when not one person signed up for it. Which one? You guessed it "Scripture Memory." It was an embarrassment to the leader to discover his workshop had been canceled for lack of interest. Even though he had prayed diligently and prepared thoroughly, no one signed up. How do I know? I've had it happen to me. So I would bundle up my notes and my handouts and my transparencies and quietly slip into the back row of a well-attended, exciting workshop conducted by a colleague. And it didn't do much for my self-image when someone asked, "How did your workshop go?" and I would have to answer, "No one came."

Scripture memory seems to be the least popular form of Scripture intake. Just why do you think this is so? What is it about Scripture memory that turns people off? Could it be that we have been led to believe that Scripture memory is not for people like you and me? Could it be that somewhere we have gotten the idea that Scripture memory is just for children?

In my own church we have made Scripture memory a vital part of the life of our Sunday School. A little child showing up for class on Sunday morning meets the Scripture Memory Lady sitting just outside the classroom door. She welcomes the child with a friendly smile and asks, "Did you memorize your verse for Sunday School this morning?" When the child says, "Yes," and recites the verse, the Scripture Memory Lady puts a gold star on the chart beside the child's name. There is no lady outside the door of my class.

Are we quietly convincing ourselves that Scripture memory is for kids? But think with me for a moment. Who was it who wrote, "How can a young man cleanse his way? By taking heed according to Your Word . . . Your Word I have hidden in my heart, that I might not sin against You" (Psalm 119:9, 11). Was it a child who wrote those words? Or were they written exclusively *for* children? No. These are words of David, the King of Israel, and one of the greatest military leaders the world has ever known. These are the words of a man who discovered the power of the Word of God lodged in his heart.

Who was it who wrote, "And these words which I command you today shall be in your heart"? (Deuteronomy 6:6) They are the words of Moses, the man who led an entire nation to freedom. And who encouraged us all to write the Word of God on the tables of our hearts? It was Solomon, one of the wisest of men. The practice of Scripture memory is not only for children, but for you and me as well.

The Benefits of Scripture Memory

Quite possibly one of the primary reasons why Scripture memory is not embraced enthusiastically is that people do not know the marvelous benefits of writing the Word of God on their hearts. Let's look at a few.

• Scripture memory helps us to keep from sinning against the Lord. Dawson Trotman, the founder of the Navigators had a little saying that he shared with us. He said, "God's Word will keep you from sin or sin will keep you from God's Word." You recall we have already looked at David's testimony in this regard when he said, "Your Word I have hidden in my heart, that I might not sin against You" (Psalm 119:11). You and I do not want to sin against God. As we walk with Him day by day, we earnestly desire to be moment by moment in sweet communion and fellowship with Him. But we have a problem. I identify with the hymn writer who wrote, "Prone to wander, Lord, I feel it, prone to leave the God I love." But if we lay up the Word of God in our hearts, the blessed and powerful Holy Spirit of God can take those words and enable us to live under their influence. So if we really and truly do not want to sin against God, we will saturate our hearts and lives with His Word.

• Scripture memory is an aid to meditation. Now I realize that some of you may be saying to yourselves, "What's so great about that?" And my answer would be, "Plenty!" The promises God makes to the person who will consistently meditate on the Word of God are so staggering that we have a hard time believing them.

• Scripture memory enables us to have the Word of God ready for us at a moment's notice. The Word of God is the sword of the Spirit (Ephesians 6:17). And if we do not have the Word of God memorized and ready for instantaneous use, we have a severe spiritual handicap. Why is that so? If you look carefully at the armor of the Christian in Ephesians 6, you discover that all the parts of the armor except the sword of the Spirit are defensive. The Sword of the Spirit is the only weapon that can be used both defensively and offensively as well. Our Lord's use of the Scriptures when attacked by Satan is a clear illustration of what you and I must do when tempted. The example of Christ should be sufficient incentive for us to fortify ourselves with God's Word so that we have it available for use when the devil attacks.

What further motivation could we possibly need? Think of it! When our hearts are filled with God's Word, we can defend ourselves against the onslaughts of the enemy and win the battle with the same power in which Jesus placed His trust. But if we launch into the battle with purely human strength and wisdom, without the Spirit's sword, we are heading for defeat.

• Scripture memory helps us to have an answer when someone comes for advice and counsel. Note Proverbs 15:23, "A man has joy by the answer of his mouth, and word spoken in due season, how good it is!" Some years ago a young man came to me for advice. He had graduated from the Air Force Academy and was pursuing a career as an officer teaching R.O.T.C. at a school on the East Coast. He had recently been approached by some zealous Christian workers urging him to give up his career as an Air Force officer and come and join them as a full-time worker in the ministry to which God had called them. They told him that he could either do that, or live his life as a second-class citizen in the kingdom of God. It seems that they thought that unless you were a full-time Christian worker, you were really a nobody.

After a rather lengthy explanation of all this, he asked, "LeRoy, what do you think?" My answer was, "It doesn't really matter what I think. What really matters is what God says." I suggested we open our Bibles to Ephesians 4 and read verses 11 and 12. After we had done that I asked him a few questions. "Do you believe God called you into the service?" He believed God had done that. I then asked, "Do you believe you can serve God in the Air Force?" He thought he could. In fact, he told me about some men he had led to Christ and some new Christians who were in his Bible study.

As we discussed his situation, I pointed out that as far as I could tell he was doing exactly what God wanted him to do, and that certainly was not second-class service performed by a second-class citizen in God's kingdom. He was serving God as a worker in His ministry and was being used by the Holy Spirit to build up the body of Christ, both numerically and in depth. I am happy to say he is still active in the Lord's work while serving Him as a full colonel at an overseas Air Force base. In fact, he has recently been asked to give his testimony to a gathering of Air Force officers from another nation.

Rather than live as a second-class citizen as was predicted, he has been used by God to minister to people in places where full-time Christian workers are unable to go. So, remember, when people have a need and you know an answer from the Bible to help meet their need, you experience great joy. Therefore, the more Scripture you have memorized, the wider the variety of needs God can enable you to meet.

A friend of mine tells the story of two girls who had been memorizing Scripture rather faithfully but had stopped. He asked one of the girls a question. "What will you do if a friend comes to you with a problem and you have nothing from the Scriptures to share with her?" "Well," she replied, "I guess I'll be in trouble." The other girl thought for a minute and then replied, "No, the friend who comes to you for help will be in trouble." God wants His people to be ready with an answer for those in need of spiritual counsel. "Have not I written to you excellent things of counsels and knowledge, that I may make you know the certainty of the words of truth; that you may answer words of truth to those who send to you?" (Proverbs 22:20-21) Here we learn that God has given us His excellent Word that we might have a firm grasp on that Word — know the *certainty* of the Word of truth — and that we might be able to share His Word with others who are in need of help.

● Scripture memory provides a good supply of the Word of truth that the Holy Spirit may bring to my remembrance. I recall being in a meeting many years ago where Dawson Trotman was speaking on the subject of Scripture memory. At the end of his sermon, he asked if there were any questions. A man spoke up and said he didn't think Scripture memory was necessary because Jesus promised that the Holy Spirit would bring the Scriptures to our remembrance when we needed them. If we were witnessing to someone and needed a verse, the Holy Spirit would cause us to remember it. Dawson's answer was, "If you have never *learned* the verse, how would it be possible for the Holy Spirit to help you *recall* the verse?"

The Holy Spirit sealed this truth to my mind from Proverbs 22:18. "For it is a pleasant thing if you keep them within you; let them all be fixed upon your lips." It is my responsibility to put the Word of God within me through Scripture memory and to keep these verses fresh through systematic review. When I do this, the verses will be fixed upon my lips by the Holy Spirit. If I do my part, the Holy Spirit will do His. We can count on His faithfulness. Can He count on us to provide a good supply of the Word of truth for Him to bring to our remembrance?

• Scripture memory keeps our minds on Christ. Isaiah 26:3 says, "You will keep him in perfect peace, whose mind is stayed on You, because he trusts in You." I have learned that I can be in turmoil, with the winds of adversity and heartache raging around my soul, but if my mind is fixed on Jesus, I can have perfect peace within.

• Scripture memory helps us set priorities. Some time ago I asked my children what their friends were giving their lives to. They came up with a list of five things, and at the top of the list, by a wide margin, was the accumulation of wealth. Now there is nothing wrong with having money. In fact, God may give a person great wealth, as He did to David and Solomon. The problem comes when we fix our minds on riches and not on God. If we do that, we will go through life unsatisfied and discontented. The Bible says, "He who loves silver will not be satisfied with silver" (Ecclesiastes 5:10). And listen to the admonition of the Apostle Paul, "Those who desire to be rich fall into temptation and a snare and into many foolish and harmful lusts which drown men in destruction and perdition. For the love of money is a root of all kinds of evil, for which some have strayed from the faith in their greediness, and pierced themselves through with many sorrows" (1 Timothy 6:9-10). If a person has those few verses memorized, when he is tempted to get his eyes on the dollar sign, the Holy Spirit has a powerful warning device to remind him of the danger of his ways.

• Scripture memory helps us be encouragers. We all need encouragement from time to time. And the problem is that the people who need a word of encouragement are not always sitting in my study where I have various translations of the Bible and devotional books from which I could read an appropriate paragraph. No, all too often those people are out there in the hurly-burly of life, and if I am to share a word from the Lord it will have to be a memorized word.

A few weeks ago I met a man and his wife who were in a ministry to children. They were discouraged, downcast, and tired, and they wondered if they were doing any good. I reminded them that today there is an army on the march that will—should the Lord tarry—eventually take over every seat in the Supreme Court, every seat in the House of Representatives and Senate, every pulpit in the land, every judge's bench, the presidency of the United States, and will become chief executive officer of every corporation in America. That army is called children. And the kind of world they make will be determined by the kind of job we do in teaching them. I could see my friends pepping up a bit, as they realized afresh the importance of their work. As we talked the Lord brought to mind Galatians 6:9, "And let not us grow weary while doing good, for in due season we shall reap if we do not lose heart." When we parted I could see that the Spirit of God had used His Word to encourage them.

The Method of Scripture Memory

We've just looked at good reasons to begin the practice of Scripture memory. We've considered the *why*. Now let's look at the *how*.

• Determine to do it and set a goal to shoot for. I like to begin my stated goal with the words, "By the grace of God, I will." For me that takes it out of the realm of human endeavor and declares my dependence on God. By the grace of God I will have the eleventh chapter of the Book of Hebrews memorized by the end of summer. Or, by the grace of God I will memorize two verses each week until Christmas. Pray for God's help. Remember the promise, "I can do all things through Christ who strengthens me" (Philippians 4:13).

• Memorize the verses word perfectly. It is helpful if you memorize from the same translation you use for your daily reading. Select a good, clear, accurate translation and memorize the verses exactly as they are written. In his commentary on the Sword of the Spirit, in Ephesians 6:17, R.C.H. Lenski sets forth a strong and convincing argument for memorizing "word perfectly." He points out that the Word of God is powerful because it is the very utterance of God. It is the word that proceeds out of the mouth of God. It is the Sword of the Spirit that is so deadly in striking down the foe of God and of man. He then goes on to say, "When we use it in our battle, we are to use it only as 'God's utterance.' Any alteration takes the power and the edge off this Sword." It is the Word of God that wins the victory over Satan. And if we alter that Word through sloppy and careless memory habits, we do so at our own peril.

Through careful memory and review, the Spirit of God will keep our verses sharp, as any good sword should be. Let us then be diligent to arm ourselves with the very Word of God in order that we might have this weapon of supernatural power available at a moment's notice.

• Memorize Scripture during times that you normally waste. Early in my Christian life, I was taught to redeem the time in this way. Every day when I walked to work at the Sears store on Lake Street in Minneapolis, I carried my little Scripture memory verse pack with me. I would either spend the time memorizing a new verse or reviewing the verses I had already learned. Years later I found out that one of the most famous men who ever lived had the same practice. William Wilberforce (1759–1883) was a member of the House of Parliament and a prominent figure in London society. He devoted his life to the abolition of the slave trade and against strong opposition was eventually successful in passing a bill that outlawed slavery—just three days before his death. During much of his life he lived with criticism, threats, and ridicule. But he had a practice that kept his mind at peace. In the midst of the stir and turmoil of a political crisis in 1819, he wrote in his diary—"Walked from Hyde Park corner repeating the 119th Psalm in great comfort."

● Many have found it helpful for another person to listen to their Scripture verses to check them for accuracy. Scores of business and professional men phone each other long distance to make sure their memory partners are getting their verses "word perfect."

● The Topical Memory System has proven to be a helpful tool for people all over the world, to get them started in Scripture memory. This system can be purchased at your local Bible bookstore.

Encouragement from the Word

As we close this chapter let's look at two passages of Scripture. The first is Proverbs 4:4, "He also taught me, and said to me: 'Let your heart retain My words; keep My commands, and live.' " These are important words from a father to his son. And they are even more important when they come from our Heavenly Father. We must retain His words by lodging them in our heart.

The second is Proverbs 4:20-21, "My son, give attention to my words; incline your ear to my sayings. Do not let them depart from your eyes; keep them in the midst of your heart." Here again we see that if it is important to heed the words of an earthly father, it is imperative that we do the same with the Word of God. In his commentary on this passage Matthew Henry said,

We must have a continual regard to the Word of God, and endeavor that it may be always ready to us. The sayings of wisdom must be our principles by which we must govern ourselves, our monitors to warn us to duty and danger; and therefore,

• We must receive them readily; "Incline thine ear to them (v. 20) humbly bow to them, diligently listen to them." The attentive hearing of the Word of God is a good sign of a work of grace begun in the heart, and a good means of carrying it on. It is to be hoped that those are resolved to do their duty who are inclined to know it.

• We must retain them carefully; (v. 21) we must lay them before us as a rule; "Let them not depart from thine eyes; view them, review them, and in everything aim to conform to them." We must lodge them within us, as a commanding principle, the influences of which are diffused throughout the whole man; "Keep them in the midst of thine heart, as things dear to thee, and which thou art afraid of losing." Let the Word of God be written in the heart, and that which is written there will remain.

Chapter 6

THE FELLOWSHIP
OF BELIEVERS

A few years ago when my wife Virginia and I were
in London, our good friend David Limebear took us sightseeing. We had been at an evangelism committee meeting at
a downtown church named All Souls Langham Place where
David is a member. He wanted to take us to Trafalgar
Square to let us see the statue of Lord Nelson at night. It
was an inspiring sight to see him standing there in the spot-
lights. As I walked around the base of the column, I got four
different views of Nelson. From the north I could see certain features that I couldn't see from the south, the east,
and the west, and so on around the square. A different
angle revealed different features.

People view Christian fellowship from different angles.
For some, fellowship means having two or three couples
over to their house for barbequed chicken and Scrabble. Or,
a Sunday School class can meet in the fellowship hall for a
ham dinner and a little fun and cap off the evening with a
few lighthearted songs. For others, it's a weekly meeting
with a Bible study group. Some gather to pray for the missionaries the church has sponsored, while others look forward to the Sunday School picnic out at the state park

where they can go for a boat ride, play shuffleboard, and where the hardier ones can organize a softball game. The word *fellowship* can take on a variety of meanings and center on everything from chocolate chip cookies and Kool-Aid to an evening of prayer for the troubled spots of the world.

One Concern

It was during a visit to London that the Lord brought to my mind the *first* vital aspect of Christian fellowship. A hurricane had recently blown through the British Isles and the marks of destruction were still evident. One of the most unusual reports about the hurricane damage was from a forest not far from London. Every tree had been knocked down. Not just *many* of the trees or even *most* of the trees, but *every* tree had been uprooted and was flat on the ground. The scientists who studied this were absolutely amazed. How could that have happened? During a hurricane you expect to see some damage in a forest, but never anything like this. So a group of the scientists went out to the forest to see if they could determine a cause.

What they discovered was that when those trees were planted, someone had made a terrible mistake. The trees were planted just a little too far apart so that the roots of one tree could not get entangled with the roots of another and thus support one another. Each tree stood there as a separate entity, and when that unusually strong wind swept through the forest, over they all went.

We need each other. We need each other's love and concern and prayers. And if a person has no good solid biblical fellowship with his brothers and sisters in Christ, but tries to go it alone, at some point he will run into trouble. God never intended for us to hold ourselves aloof from the care and concern of our fellow Christians. In fact, the Lord likens us to a body where "the eye cannot say to the hand, 'I have no need of you' " (1 Corinthians 12:21). At the Navigator Conference Center in Colorado Springs we have a rule: don't go hiking alone. You might fall off one of the giant boulders and sprain your ankle, or you might be bitten by a rattlesnake. It's fun to take a walk up Queen's Canyon and inspiring to climb up to Dawson Trotman's grave on Razorback Ridge, but it is always good to go with a partner. If something happens to one of you, the other one is there to help. The Bible says, "Two are better than one, because they have a good reward for their labor. For if they fall one will lift up his companion. But woe to him who is alone when he falls, for he has no one to help him up" (Ecclesiastes 4:9-10).

Yes, and pity the man or woman for whom no one prays. And pity the man or woman for whom no one is concerned. One of the most meaningful aspects of our Sunday School class is the care and concern segment, where we are brought news of fellow members who need our prayers, and where we are encouraged to visit them, pray for them, and send them a letter or a greeting card that expresses our care and concern. One of God's earliest observations concerning the man He had created was, "It is not good that man should be alone" (Genesis 2:18). To help with this aloneness, God has given us not only loving companionship but Christian fellowship as well. The first 3,000 converts "continued steadfastly in the apostles' doctrine and fellowship, in breaking of bread, and in prayers . . . So continuing daily with one accord in the temple, and breaking bread from house to house, they ate their food with gladness and simplicity of heart, praising God and having favor with all the people" (Acts 2:42, 46-47). What a picture of happy, devoted fellowship. Here was a band of prayerful, sacrificial, joyful Christians who were experiencing the fullness of Christ-centered fellowship, with no one wanting to stand off by himself alone.

One Heart and Soul

A *second* vital aspect of Christian fellowship can be seen in Acts 4:32, "Now the multitude of those who believed were of one heart and one soul." They not only were concerned for each other, with a God-given desire to help hold each other up during times of stress and trouble, but they had actually become part of each other's lives. Let me illustrate that profound truth. When I was in my last year in high school in Neola, Iowa, I got a job in a bakery cleaning the oven and the pots and pans. This was during World War II, and one day the baker received some terrible news. His son Wade had been captured by the Nazi army during one of the battles in North Africa. Herb, the baker, fell apart. He did not have the strength or the will to go on. He said he was going to close the bakery indefinitely. He had no more desire to bake the bread, the donuts, and sweet rolls. For the time being, he was through. So I went to the girl who waited on the customers in the front of the store and asked, "How would you like to keep this bakery open? I know how to bake bread. I've watched Herb make pies and cakes, donuts, and sweet rolls. Let's try to keep the bakery going." She said, "Okay," and so we began. Then one day the Ladies Aid Society came in the store to buy refreshments for their monthly meeting. After looking everything over, they settled on chocolate donuts. Now I knew that's what they would do. I had watched them before. After making a few kind remarks about other things, they always settled on chocolate donuts. They were all wild about them. And for that reason Herb kept lots of chocolate on hand.

So I began the process. I made the donuts and then fired up the double boiler to melt the chocolate to dunk the donuts in. I broke off large pieces of chocolate and tossed them into the double boiler. These large, jagged pieces of chocolate just sat there until the boiler got warm and the hunks of chocolate began to melt and run to the bottom of the pan. Soon the pieces of chocolate had become a warm, gooey, sloppy mess in the bottom of the boiler. And that's a picture of fellowship. Fellowship is not simply all of us in the same building, occasionally making some contact with each other, like jagged pieces of chocolate in the same pan. No, fellowship results as the blessed Holy Spirit of God begins to warm our hearts toward each other, and we soon actually become part of each other with one heart, one soul, and one mind.

Our Body

A *third* ingredient of Christian fellowship can be found in Paul's letter to the Ephesians where he says that from Christ "the whole body, joined and knit together by what every joint supplies ... causes growth of the body for the edifying of itself in love" (4:16). Here we learn four great truths.

● The whole body is dependent on Christ.

● All the parts of the body must be joined to each other.

● Each part of the body must do the work it was designed for.

● If the body functions this way, it will grow.

During my years at Northwestern College in Minneapolis, my parents lived in Omaha, Nebraska. I had made friends with a guy whose home was also in Omaha and he had a car. Not much of a car, but it ran, and he offered to drive Virginia and me and our baby to Omaha during the school breaks. We accepted his offer gladly and made several trips together. One day we were on our way to Omaha when we heard a loud noise in the engine. We pulled into a filling station and the attendant told us we had thrown a rod. Neither Scotty or I knew what that meant, so the attendant explained that we couldn't drive the car until it was fixed. But we determined to give it a try; and by driving around thirty miles per hour, and keeping lots of heavy oil in the engine, we made it. When we arrived home, Scotty told us he was going to repair the engine himself. He had a plan. He would get some tools, take the engine apart, replace the broken, bent, and scarred pieces with others he could get at the junkyard, reassemble the engine and see what happened. So he did. When he removed a part that was damaged, he put a number on it, and laid it on the big front porch of his parents' home. Soon the engine was completely apart and the broken parts were all in a row on the front porch, each with a number. He took his gunnysack filled with defective parts to the junkyard, replaced them with good used parts, reassembled the engine, turned the key and— much to Scotty's surprise and delight—the engine ran!

Now let me ask you a question. When the good, used parts were all put in their numbered place on the porch, were they together? Well, yes, sort of. But they didn't *do* anything. They were just lying there, all in rows, perfectly good parts but accomplishing nothing. It wasn't until they were put in the engine, with each part functioning as it was designed to, that they could produce the power to run the car.

The fellowship of believers is not only a matter of holding each other up, or becoming part of each other through care and concern and prayer. In addition to those things each of us has a work to do, a job to perform, a task to accomplish. And until we give ourselves to that task, the whole body is out of kilter. Not one of us is unimportant. We all need to roll up our sleeves and pitch in with our whole heart. Until we do that, the picture is not complete.

Shortly before the 1975 war in Lebanon got really hot,

my wife and I were there on a preaching tour. We were staying with friends in their fourth floor apartment near the downtown section. It was a beautiful apartment, and one of its outstanding features was its lovely tile floor. But something had happened that spoiled its beauty. A previous renter had apparently dropped something heavy and broken one of the tiles. And with that tile missing, the picture was not complete. Fellowship is more than just eating cookies together. It is all of us marching arm in arm toward the goal, making our contributions to the kingdom of Jesus Christ.

Our Mission

A *fourth* illustration of a vital ingredient of Christian fellowship can be found in the life of Demas, a co-laborer of the Apostle Paul. He was listed by Paul alongside such stalwarts as Luke, the beloved physician. But something happened to this man that caused him to abandon the mission of Christ. Paul puts it simply, "Demas has forsaken me, having loved this present world" (2 Timothy 4:10). Here is a cause for concern for all of us. Remember, Demas was one of Paul's closest associates. And we are reminded by what Demas did that we are all vulnerable. Demas was no weak beginner; he was a mature disciple. So what can we do? Is there something that God has provided that the Holy Spirit can use to keep us warm toward the things of the Lord?

Some years ago my wife and I were speaking at a week-long collegiate conference at a mountain retreat center in France. One evening the students built a big bonfire and had a wiener roast. I placed my hotdog on a stick and roasted it. Later I cooked some marshmallows for dessert. The fire was blazing and the flames were leaping when the bell rang to call us to the evening meeting. I wondered how they would put out the fire, since I saw no water or buckets of sand nearby to extinguish the flames. To satisfy my curiosity, I waited to see what they would do. I didn't have long to wait. A young man wearing heavy boots walked up to the fire and gave it a hearty kick. One blazing log rolled this way, another that way, and soon they all were scattered. In minutes the flames subsided, and the logs lost their glow. But as long as they were in a tight cluster they would have kept burning.

This illustrates the importance of maintaining a close fellowship with our brothers and sisters in Christ. If we wander off by ourselves, we are in danger of falling into the devil's snare. Most animal predators look to attack one that has strayed from the flock. Remember the warning given by the Apostle Peter, "Be sober, be vigilant; because your adversary the devil walks about like a roaring lion, seeking whom he may devour" (1 Peter 5:8).

One Identity

In closing this chapter, let me list for you a few things I have found that God can use to draw hearts together.

• One is a Bible Study group made up of a half-dozen people who gather together to discuss the Scriptures. Keep the discussion Bible-based and Christ-centered.

• The second thing I have found to be a real "heart binder" is a weekly prayer gathering where a few people with the work of Christ on their hearts meet to pray for the needs of their families, their church, and the work of Christ around the world. There are a number of very fine prayer guides that keep you abreast of what the Spirit of God is doing in various places around the globe.

• The third thing is having fun together. Early in my Christian life I heard a leader of a worldwide Bible society say that the highest form of identification is having fun together. God can use parties, picnics, and sporting events to deepen our friendships. Try to arrange for your Sunday School class to take over the local pizza parlor, the high school swimming pool, or the bowling alley.

• And lastly, try to arrange for your group to spend some time witnessing in the mall or going from door to door in the neighborhood with the Gospel. Getting out together in the battle for souls will draw your hearts closer, and being in the battle together can make for a deepened sense of fellowship.

Chapter 7

THE CHURCH

Their eyebrows always go up. Some people's mouths drop open. They may get a startled look on their faces. They never fail to show—and sometimes express—surprise when I say I would rather worship God on Sunday morning in my home church than anything else I can think of. I suppose there are many who don't believe me, but it's true. If you offer me the opportunity to go snorkeling in the South China Sea, or gaze at Paris on a bright spring morning from atop the Eiffel Tower, or go shopping in Hong Kong, or ski in the Swiss Alps, or attend a concert in the Sydney Opera House, or take the grandkids to Disneyland, or go to my home church and worship the Lord—I'll go to church.

Now to be honest with you, I have not always had a love for the church. In my early days of Christian service, I could take the church or leave it. It was sort of a necessary nuisance. My heart was on the college campuses and the military bases. Reaching young men for Christ was my passion, and I gave myself unreservedly to the proclamation of the Gospel to servicemen and the university students. Because my wife and I had young children, we attended church and Sunday School regularly, but it was primarily for the sake of our kids. But over the years I have noticed a remarkable change in my attitude toward the church; it now has a much deeper place in my heart and prayers.

If you are helping young Christians learn to walk with the Lord and serve Him, be patient with them in their attitude toward the church. Pray for them, keep them involved, and let the Holy Spirit woo them to a wholehearted involvement in and love for His church. And if you are a young Christian and eager to grow, let me share with you some of the things about the church that have proven to be so helpful to me in my Christian growth. First of all, it is a place where I can hear a man of God preach the Word of God. I have found this to be an invaluable and exciting means of taking in the Word of God. The preacher spends many hours preparing his message to us, and he always seems to turn up something new and fresh in the passage he is expounding. Even if I have studied the passage a dozen times, he seems to see things that totally escaped me, or he sees things from an entirely different angle. We are fortunate in our church to have small 3x5 cards in the pew pocket in front of where we are sitting. That makes it very easy to take notes on the message and discuss it on the way home.

Let me remind you that there are four means of Scripture intake. Through the preached Word we hear it. Through the printed page we read it. Through various methods we study it, and through Scripture memory we write it on the table of the heart. And if we eliminate any of these from our lives, we do so at our peril. Each one has its own strengths, and that is certainly true of hearing it proclaimed. Seven times in the Book of Revelation we read these words, "He who has an ear, let him hear what the Spirit says to the churches." And remember, the Spirit of God uses the man of God to bring the Word of God to the people of God. So one reason why I like to hear the Word preached is that I see the passage from a new angle.

A second reason I enjoy hearing the Word is that it peps me up and bolsters my faith. Many times I have arrived at church discouraged and tired. The choir bursts forth with an admonition to rise up and put our armor on. I say to myself, "In my condition, I should be putting my pajamas on." Then we all rise and sing, "When morning gilds the skies, my heart awaking cries, may Jesus Christ be praised," and I am on the road to recovery. Next comes a missions report that tells us of exciting things God is doing in some remote corner of the earth, and by now I am with it. I have fully recovered and am ready to hear a good, sound exposition of the Bible.

In worship I am transformed from a bleary-eyed, discouraged child of God into a fired-up Christian ready to tackle another week. I am grateful for the promise of Jeremiah 3:15, "And I will give you shepherds according to My heart, who will feed you with knowledge and understanding." Therefore, "I was glad when they said to me, 'Let us go into the house of the Lord' " (Psalm 122:1).

The Encouragement of Fellowship

When we leave the morning worship service, my wife and I head for our Sunday School class. We joined the class in 1955 and have enjoyed the fellowship and Bible teaching for lo these many years. The members of the class are the people we really know in the church. Our kids have grown up together and we have grown older together. So naturally it is the Sunday School class that provides a sense of oneness and love that we would not have if we went only to the worship service. It is in class that we keep current with the needs of the sick and hurting. Since it was in a Sunday School class that Virginia and I met the people who were responsible for our conversion to Christ, it has been a natural thing for us to attend Sunday School. I suppose some of you may be saying, "Well, whoopie do! LeRoy attends Sunday School. Big deal." Well, no, it's not much of a big deal. But that simple decision we made years ago to attend both church and Sunday School has resulted in our receiving an extra hour of Bible training almost every week for over forty years, and that *is* significant. If you want to experience the maximum spiritual growth in your life, my advice would be for you to not only be faithful in your attendance at worship but also to seek out a good Sunday School class. It won't provide all that you need, but God will use it to make a real contribution to your spiritual well-being.

The Power of Praise

One of the most meaningful aspects of worship is the joy that floods our hearts as we stand together as a congregation and praise the Lord in song. From time to time I receive invitations to go to other cities and speak to gatherings of God's people. This can take the form of a weekend discipleship conference or simply to minister the Word at the regular Sunday services. In visiting these churches, I have become aware of the fact that praise is being given an increasing role in the life of the church. Some years ago praise was considered merely a warm-up to help get us into the real thing. But more and more we are learning of the tremendous power of praise, and its true place as we gather to worship.

Praise is a form of prayer. God says, "Whoever offers praise glorifies Me" (Psalm 50:23). The prophet said, "O Lord, You are my God. I will exalt You, I will praise Your Name" (Isaiah 25:1). There have been times in my life when the situation seemed so hopeless I just couldn't pray. So, I would begin praising the Lord. I would praise Him for who He is, the Creator of heaven and earth; I would praise Him for His matchless power and amazing grace, for His love and mercy and goodness. Soon the cloud would lift, my spirits would soar, and I would be on top again. When things get too tough for prayer, try praise. If you and I reflect frequently on the nature of God, His power, righteousness, and love, and then think that in love He would stoop to die on a cross for our sins, this should inspire us to exclaim, "O God, who am I to be so blessed?" This should cause us to cast ourselves at His feet in thanksgiving and praise, in a spirit of true humility. The desire of God's heart is that we live before Him in beautiful fellowship, full of devotion and praise.

A life of praise, then, is a life occupied with God Himself, not His gifts, not what He has done for us, but who He is as we stand in awe at the splendor of His person. The Prophet Isaiah paints a truly remarkable picture of God. "For thus says the High and Lofty One who inhabits eternity, whose name is Holy: I dwell in the high and holy place, with him who has a contrite and humble spirit, to revive the heart of the humble, and to revive the heart of the contrite ones" (Isaiah 57:15). Here God is portrayed as "the High and Lofty One, who inhabits eternity, whose name is Holy."

Note that His dwelling place is eternity. And in light of that fact, there is a rather mysterious reference made by David concerning the habitation of God. He says, "But You are holy, who inhabit the praises of Israel" (Psalm 22:3). Does that mean that when a congregation of humble and contrite children of God gather and lift their voices to praise and worship this High and Lofty One whose name is Holy, that the eternal God descends from His lofty habitation and stoops to fill the sanctuary with His holy presence and awesome power and takes up residence in the praises of His people? Yes! God inhabits praise.

The power of praise is clearly seen in the story of one of the strangest battles of the Old Testament, recorded in 2 Chronicles 20. King Jehoshaphat had learned of a powerful enemy heading his way bent on war. In his preparation for battle, he offered one of the most humble prayers recorded in Scripture. "O our God, will You not judge them? For we have no power against this great multitude that is coming against us; nor do we know what to do, but our eyes are upon You" (v. 12). To reassure the king, the Lord sent a message by a Levite named Jahaziel with these words:

Listen, all you of Judah, and you inhabitants of Jerusalem, and you, King Jehoshaphat! Thus says the Lord to you: "Do not be afraid nor dismayed because of this great multitude, for the battle is not yours, but God's. Tomorrow go down against them. They will surely come up by the ascent of Ziz, and you will find them at the end of the brook before the Wilderness of Jeruel. You will not need to fight in this battle. Position yourselves, stand still, and see the salvation of the Lord, who is with you, O Judah and Jerusalem. Do not fear, or be dismayed; tomorrow go out against them, for the Lord is with you."

And Jehoshaphat bowed his head with his face to the ground, and all Judah and the inhabitants of Jerusalem bowed before the Lord, worshiping the Lord. Then the Levites of the children of the Kohathities, and of the children of the Korhites, stood up to praise the Lord God of Israel with voices loud and high.

And they rose early in the morning and went out into the Wilderness of Tekoa; and as they went out, Jehoshaphat stood and said, "Hear me, O Judah, and you inhabitants of Jerusalem: Believe in the Lord your God, and you shall be established; believe His prophets, and you shall prosper."

And when he consulted with the people, he appointed those who should sing to the Lord, and who should praise the beauty of holiness, as they went out before the army and were saying, "Praise the Lord, for His mercy endures forever."

Now when they began to sing and to praise, the Lord set ambushes against the people of Ammon, Moab, and Mount Seir, who had come against Judah; and they were defeated (vv. 15-22).

When you enter the sanctuary and sing the hymns, think about the power that resides in your praise.

The Privilege of Giving

At some point in your Sunday morning worship, you will be given the high privilege of placing in the offering plate God's tithes and your offerings. Over the years I have observed an interesting fact. The person who learns early in his Christian life the grace of generous giving unto the Lord is greatly blessed by God and in turn becomes a blessing. Let me share with you a number of key Scripture passages that deal with both the *why* and the *how* of Christ-honoring stewardship.

In Luke 16:1-2 Jesus introduces us to a steward who wasted what his master had entrusted to him. "There was a certain rich man who had a steward, and an accusation was brought to him that this man had wasted his goods. So he called him and said to him, "What is this I hear about you? Give an account of your stewardship; for you can no longer be steward."

We can see in this passage that his lack of faithful stewardship was highly displeasing to his master. We can be led into poor stewardship by four things: *extravagance, covet-*

ousness, greed, and *ignorance,* and thus be unable to obey this clear teaching: "Withhold not good from them to whom it is due, when it is in the power of thine hand to do it." Whenever we are able, we should help those who are in need.

Extravagance often leads to our inability to give generously unto the Lord and fulfill our responsibilities as good stewards of that which God has placed in our care. I remember a university student who came to a weekend conference where a missionary was speaking. As this young college student listened, the greater his desire grew to help the missionary financially. But he had a problem. Just the week before, he had purchased a car. And not just any old car. It was a brand-new luxury automobile with every possible accessory. It didn't just have a radio—it had the best radio money could buy. It didn't just have a front and rear speaker for the radio and tape deck—it had speakers in the dashboard, in the doors and back by the rear window. It didn't just have a good engine—it had an engine that enabled him to pass anything on the road. To put it simply, it was a much more expensive automobile than any college freshman needs. By any measurement, his purchase was an act of extravagance. Huge car payments for years to come hung around his neck like an anchor. And there he stood wishing he could make a financial investment in reaching souls for Christ through the missionary, but he was unable to do so. His *extravagance* rendered him unable to fulfill his responsibilities of a good steward.

Covetousness can also be a big problem for many. Early on in the life of His people God saw the need to lay down the law, "You shall not covet" (Exodus 20:17). Essentially, covetousness accuses God of mismanagement. Since God owns everything, He decides what to allot to you and to others. When we covet, we are arguing with God about the way He is managing His affairs. The antidote to covetousness is giving. "Give, and it will be given to you, a good measure, pressed down, shaken together, and running over will be put into your bosom. For with the same measure that you use, it will be measured back to you" (Luke 6:38). As Christians, we are essentially God's delivery system; we are His United Parcel Service. We deliver material things to the needy around us. Since those things often corrupt us, God is limited as to how much passes through our hands, because of our tendency to stop the flow and siphon off the abundance for ourselves. Once we have that problem licked, however, it's amazing how much of God's resources can flow through our lives. We ought to be eager for God to maximize His plan for world evangelization through us. Heaven is just bursting with blessings for those who are generous, those who do not covet. It is like a granary jammed full, just waiting to be opened so that the blessings can be spread around. Aladdin had only to rub the magic lamp and the genie appeared; Ali Baba just said, "Open Sesame!" All the Christian has to do is learn to give generously. " 'Bring all the tithes into the storehouse, that there may be food in My house, and prove Me now in this,' says the Lord of hosts, 'if I will not open for you the windows of heaven and pour out for you such blessing that there will not be room enough to receive it' " (Malachi 3:10).

A third enemy to generous giving is *greed*. Someone asked a wealthy man how much money it would take to satisfy his desire for money. He said, "Just a little bit more."

A fourth enemy to becoming a generous giver is *ignorance*. We should become aware of what God is doing around the world and where the needs are. Our Sunday School class supports a number of missionaries, and every Sunday morning the class member who is responsible to keep us up to date on the missionaries' health, financial needs, and ministries reads a recent report from one of the missionaries so that we can see our gifts in action. The more you know about the worldwide mission of Christ, the greater joy you will have in giving.

Some months ago my wife and I had the privilege of giving toward the purchase of a new airplane to be used by the Wycliffe Bible Translators in Loma Linda, Colombia, South America. A few years ago we flew to Loma Linda over the Andes Mountains with the Wycliffe people in an old plane that went into service sometime around the late 1930s or early 1940s. The passengers were Virginia and myself and 100 turkeys. We made it safe and sound, of course; but when we heard they were trying to replace that very old airplane with a new one, we immediately sent some money to help. And we would not have known about the need if we hadn't read about it in a Wycliffe magazine. Today there are numerous magazines and prayer reminders that God can use to keep us abreast of the working of His Spirit throughout the world—what the needs are, how we can have a part and obey the command of Scripture, "Honor the Lord with your possessions, and with the firstfruits of all your increase" (Proverbs 3:9).

The Apostle Paul had much to say regarding generous giving. He told the Corinthians,

> But this I say: He who sows sparingly will reap also sparingly and he who sows bountifully will also reap bountifully. So let each one give as he purposes in his heart, not grudgingly, or of necessity; for God loves a cheerful giver. And God is able to make all grace abound toward you, that you, always having all sufficiency in all things, have an abundance for every good work. As it is written: "He has dispersed abroad, He has given to the poor; His righteousness remains forever" (2 Corinthians 9:6-9).

Giving is one of the most Godlike things we can do:

"For God so loved the world that He gave His only begotten Son, that whoever believes in Him should not perish, but have everlasting life" (John 3:16). Regular church attendance then, is one of the ingredients in our spiritual growth. As we gather together to worship God, a number of wonderful things await us.

- We will hear the Word of God preached.

- We will have fellowship with fellow Christians.

- We will be reminded of the Great Commission of Jesus Christ.

- We will have opportunity to join others in praising the Lord.

- We will have opportunity to give to the Lord.
  See you in church!

Chapter 8

WITNESSING

In this chapter we consider a topic that generally ranges in popularity somewhere between a snakebite and a tough case of the flu: WITNESSING. And it is really too bad that people feel that way. As George Worrell pointed out in a workshop on witnessing many years ago, those feelings are often the result of a tragic misunderstanding of what witnessing is really all about. But there it is and we cannot deny it. I've seen big bruisers over six feet tall turn to jelly at the thought of talking to someone about Christ. I've seen highly educated people, able to hold their own in any conversation, grow pale at the prospect of mentioning the name of Jesus to a friend. I've seen people who are normally the life of the party clam up and hide when an opportunity to present the Gospel comes along.

A Tragic Misunderstanding

The reason people come down with spiritual lockjaw and find it difficult to give a word of witness is all too often due to a simple misunderstanding. To help us clear up this tragic misunderstanding, let's look at the people involved in the ministry of witnessing. The first is a *gracious and loving God* who wants all men to be saved and come to the knowledge of the truth (1 Timothy 2:4). The Apostle Peter describes this gracious loving God as the one who is "not willing that any should perish but that all should come to repentance" (2 Peter 3:9).

The second is a *person seeking the truth.* These people are everywhere — in the neighborhood where you live, down at the office or plant where you work, over at the club where you exercise — everywhere. And here is the exciting thing.

Right now the *Holy Spirit,* the third person in this saga of salvation, is working night and day to create a hunger for God in the hearts of these seeking souls and is devising means to bring these people across your path.

Therefore, the fourth person involved is a *willing witness.* Jesus said, "As the Father has sent Me, I also send you" (John 20:21). That is where you come in. That is your cue to get involved in this process. And remember this — God does not need your ability, but He does need your availability. He hunts for people who are willing to get involved.

The four people involved, then, in an effective witness are our loving, merciful, gracious *God,* an honest *seeker* after truth, the *Holy Spirit,* and a willing *witness.* And when these four meet at some divinely appointed junction, eternal business can be accomplished and a life can be transformed if the willing witness shares Christ in complete dependence on the Holy Spirit and leaves the results with God. And right there is where our tragic misunderstanding takes place. *You and I are not responsible for results.* But somehow many of us have been led to believe that if we don't actually lead the person to Christ, we have failed. Nonsense! That is completely out of our hands.

What is our job? To present the message of Christ simply and clearly. It is the Holy Spirit's ministry to convict the person of his sin and convince him of his need for Christ; so, no matter the outcome, if we have shared the Good News in complete dependence on the Holy Spirit, we can confidently leave the results to Him. Only the Holy Spirit can convict the person of his need for forgiveness. Only the Holy Spirit can convince the person that he must turn to Jesus Christ in repentance and faith. Only the Holy Spirit can lead the person to open his heart to Christ and receive Him as personal Savior and Lord. And only the Holy Spirit can create a desire in the heart of a person to find salvation in Christ. We cannot do the work of God. But we can be used of God in His work. And what is our part? It is the high privilege of sharing the message of salvation in Jesus Christ.

The Five Musts of Witnessing

A few months ago my four-year-old grandson came home from a children's meeting in a nearby church and was obviously troubled by something. Since the meeting was not sponsored by our church, our daughter-in-law wondered just what had taken place and so she asked him what had gone on. He said they had sung some songs and heard a Bible story. At that point he asked the question that was troubling him. "Mama," he said, "is it true that if a person has Jesus in his heart, he will go to heaven?" "Yes, that is true," she replied. "And is it true that if a person does not have Jesus in his heart, he will go to a real bad place and not to heaven?" "Yes, that also is true," she said. He thought about that for a minute and said, "Well, then, if that's true, we'd better tell them!" Based on the facts as he understood them, there was just one obvious conclusion: Become a willing witness to be used by the Lord to share the message of eternal salvation in Jesus Christ and help people learn the way to heaven. Let's look at five "musts" in being a willing witness.

Persevere

About twenty years after Paul entered the ministry which God gave him as an Apostle, he said, "Having obtained help from God, to this day I stand, witnessing both to small and great, saying no other things than those which the prophets and Moses said would come — that the Christ would suffer, that He would be the first to rise from the dead, and would proclaim light to the Jewish people and to the Gentiles" (Acts 26:22-23). After twenty years his burden was the same and his message was the same. He persevered in spite of countless setbacks and difficulties. He told the Corinthians,

Are they ministers of Christ? — I speak as a fool — I am more: in labors more abundant, in stripes above measure, in prisons more frequently, in deaths often. From the Jews five times I received forty stripes minus one. Three times I was beaten with rods; once I was stoned; three times I was shipwrecked; a night and a day I have been in the deep; in journeys often, in perils of waters, in perils of robbers, in perils of my own countrymen, in perils of the Gentiles, in perils of the city, in perils in the wilderness, in perils in the sea, in perils among false brethren; in weariness and toil, in sleeplessness often, in hunger and thirst, in fastings often, in cold and nakedness — beside the other things, what comes upon me daily; my deep concern for all the churches (2 Corinthians 11:23-28).

Earlier in that same letter he said, "We are hard

pressed on every side, yet not crushed; we are perplexed, but not in despair; persecuted, but not forsaken; struck down, but not destroyed—always carrying about in the body the dying of the Lord Jesus, that the life of Jesus also may be manifested in our body" (2 Corinthians 4:8-10). Yes, as a willing witness you must persevere.

Some years ago Lorne Sanny, then President of the Navigators, was invited to go to Dallas, Texas to give a series of lectures on leadership to a gathering of Wycliffe Bible Translators. Lorne asked if I would like to go along and, of course, I was more than happy to do so. We arranged to meet at the Wycliffe headquarters. So on the appointed day I boarded the plane for Dallas. In those days the way you got to Dallas from Colorado Springs was to fly to Denver and then on to Dallas. I got on the plane to Denver and sat down next to a couple on their way to Honolulu. In a few minutes we were engaged in a conversation about spiritual matters and I discovered they were both Christians, so during the eighteen-minute flight we had warm Christian fellowship. When we landed in Denver the passengers who were not going to Dallas deplaned. There were about twenty of us who stayed on board the airplane. Since we were going to be on the ground for about twenty minutes, I decided to find someone to talk to. I went down the aisle and walked up to a young guy and said, "How's it going?" "Oh, fine," he said and soon we were discussing the Gospel. He was delighted to talk about the Lord because he was a Christian who was returning from a rich spiritual retreat and was looking for someone to talk to about what he had learned.

The stewardess soon spoke into the intercom and called us back to our seats. So I sat down and waited to see who the Lord would bring along my path on our flight from Denver to Dallas. A young man got on the plane and sat down in my row. After we took off I asked, "Where are you from?" "North Dakota" he replied. "North Dakota," I said, "You must be a Lutheran." Everyone I've ever met from North Dakota is a Lutheran. "No," he said, "I'm not a Lutheran." "Is that right!" I exclaimed, "What religion are you?" It turned out he was nothing. He had no religion. At last! I thought to myself. Finally I've found someone to talk to about the message of salvation. And as it turned out, he was eager to talk about the claims of Christ. Do you recall the little saying that goes, "If at first you don't succeed, try, try, again"? In other words—don't give up. Persevere!

Be a Friendly Witness

You must not make a nuisance out of yourself. One of the most interesting passages of Scripture speaks to this point. Luke tells us in Acts 19:31 that the Apostle Paul had friends among the chief men of Asia called Asiarchs, a title given to men of high rank. One of their responsibilities was to regulate the worship of the Roman Emperor and various pagan gods. Imagine that. Paul, the most outspoken witness of his day had made friends with these men who promoted the practices of paganism. When Paul showed up they were glad to see him because he was their friend. And somehow he had earned the right to be heard among these influential men of Asia. We wonder what Paul did to win the friendship of the people. One thing we know for sure, is that he had not behaved in such a way that they hated to see him come to Ephesus. He was not considered a nuisance to be avoided.

I am often reminded of these words in Acts 19:31 when I return home from a preaching tour. I can hardly wait to sit down at the table and enjoy one of my wife's wonderful meals. My wife is an outstanding cook. If I've been out ministering among the university crowd, I have had my fill of pizza, hamburgers, tacos, hot dogs, and buckets of fried chicken. Now I am ready for a good home-cooked meal. Finally, the long awaited moment arrives. I go to the table, ask God's blessing on the food, fill my plate, and the telephone rings. The caller wants to know if I would like to install solar energy equipment in our home. I glance at my plate and the food that is getting cold and I tell him, "Thanks, but no thanks." I return to my chair, sit down, pick up my fork, and the phone rings. The caller wants to know if I would be interested in a lawn care program that he is selling. Again, it's "Thanks, but no thanks." I return to my chair and before I can pick up my fork, the phone rings. The caller wants to know if I would be interested in having aluminum siding installed to protect our home from the ravages of wind and rain and sunshine and hail and so on. I assure him we don't need any at the moment—we have just painted the house. I head back to my chair and before I can sit down, a caller wants to know if my wife and I would be interested in purchasing some property in the mountains. I suppose by now you have the idea. I wish these people would leave me alone. They have become a nuisance and I resent their intrusion. Now Christians, your witness can be like that. But not so with Paul. These Asiarchs were his friends and were happy to see him. Persevere, yes, but don't make a nuisance of yourself.

Do Not Be Controlled by Fear

Do not allow yourself to be controlled by unwarranted fear. You and I must have one controlling power over our lives and that is the control of the Holy Spirit. But unwarranted fear is an ever present danger. Some years ago my wife and I were on a two-month preaching tour throughout South America. In one of the cities we were bombarded by grafitti that urged, "Yankee Go Home." After a rather late meeting we went to our hotel, and soon we were fast asleep. Around 3 A.M., we were awakened by gunfire. There was a continuous barrage of automatic weapons, mortars, hand grenades, and small-arms fire. My wife sat up in bed and asked, "What is that?" "That's a war," I replied. "I've been in a war and I know what one sounds like. And that's a war." In my mind I could envision a couple of soldiers checking the register at the desk of the hotel, discovering that we were on the third floor, kicking the door open, demanding money or whatever they wanted. But it didn't happen. And, around 6 A.M., the war ceased. About noon the next day I said, "Let's brave it to find something to eat." We found a small restaurant and ordered some chicken. As we were eating, to our dismay the war broke out again. But the strange thing was that no one in the restaurant even looked up to see what was going on. I stopped the waiter and asked, "What is that?" He smiled and replied, "Today is the birthday of our favorite saint, and we shoot off firecrackers and other harmless explosives to celebrate our saint's birthday." My wife and I had lost most of a night's sleep worrying about what turned out to be a birthday party! Now let me ask you—was that silly? Yes, it was, but no sillier than some of the unwarranted fears that grip the hearts of people at the thought of giving a word of witness for the Lord.

Make the Message Clear

To be a good witness, you must make the message clear. Once in Boulder, Colorado, my wife and I were speaking at an evangelistic meeting on the campus of the University of Colorado. As we were walking from the meeting to our room, we passed a laundromat that had just been robbed.

The police had found the thief and began to issue instructions. "Hold it right there. Get out of the car. Slowly get out of the car. Get out now. Get down on your knees now. I said, *now.* Keep your hands up. Don't move." There could be no mistaking what the police wanted. Their message was clear.

Whenever I think of the need to make the message clear, I am reminded of the time a friend of mine, Cec Davidson, and I were in Tokyo and decided to stop at a restaurant and get a bowl of ice cream. We looked at the menu and made our order. Shortly the waitress showed up with various bowls and assorted dishes and chopsticks and other things that went with the five-course meal we had ordered. We never did get our ice cream.

A while back I was in Southern California speaking at the various colleges and universities in the area. One day I met a young man on campus wearing a strange symbol around his neck. When I inquired about it he said it identified him with a rock group. He told me the name of the group, so I asked him what their objective was. Without hesitation he said, "We are out to do two things. One, destroy the morals of the young people of America, and second, promote Satan worship." I was shocked, but later it occurred to me that he did have his message clear. He knew exactly what his objectives were and he knew how to make them clear.

Live a Holy Lifestyle

Your lifestyle must be one that glorifies Christ — one that pleases Him. You must not be conformed to the world. "But," someone asks, "what about the idea that I should adopt the lifestyle of the pagan world in order that I might win the worldling? Isn't that what the Apostle Paul taught in 1 Corinthians?"

For though I am free from all men, I have made myself a servant to all, that I might win the more, and to the Jews I became as a Jew, that I might win the Jews; to those who are under the law, as under the law, that I might win those who are under the law; to those who are without law, as without law, (being not without law toward God, but under the law toward Christ), that I might win those who are without law; to the weak I became as weak, that I might win the weak. I have become all things to all men, that I might by all means save some. Now this I do for the Gospel's sake, that I might be partaker of it with you (1 Corinthians 9:19-23).

Look at it again. "To the Jews I became as a Jew, to them who are without law, as without law. To the weak I became as weak." And then his summary: "I have become all things to all men, that I might by all means save some. Now this," he says, "I do for the Gospel's sake." Now I ask you — isn't that a license to live the lifestyle of the worldling that he might reach the worldling? My answer: No, it definitely is not. The *Wycliffe Bible Commentary* says, "While Paul was not under the law, he did not become an outlaw or lawless." In his comment on 1 Corinthians 9:22, Leon Morris says, "He sums it all up with, 'I am made all things to all men.' This does not, of course, mean that his conduct was unprincipled." No, Paul did not live like a pagan to reach the pagans.

As a matter of fact, R.C.H. Lenski in commenting on this passage points out Paul's comments have very little to do with his *lifestyle* and much to do with his *teaching style*. He points out that Paul became not a Jew, but *as* a Jew, by using *their forms of teaching* when he sought to convert them. When he was in Athens, he formulated his teaching so that it might make the strongest appeal to the Gentile mind. Paul did not, of course, live in a lawless and godless fashion when he was among Gentiles. He was and remained a Christian among the Jews. This passage is not a license to live like a pagan but to learn to communicate the message of Christ to whatever group of people you are in contact with. Living a godly life is an absolute must if you want to be a good witness for the Lord. To the Christians at Corinth, Paul gave this strong admonition. "Awake to righteousness, and do not sin; for some have not the knowledge of God. I speak this to your shame" (1 Corinthians 15:34).

Here then, are five musts if you would be a good witness for the Savior.

● Persevere. If at first you don't succeed, try, try again. It's always too soon to give up.

● Don't be a nuisance. We're out to win people, not drive them away.

● Be under the control of the Holy Spirit. Be a channel for Him.

● Make the message clear. Use words people can understand.

● Make sure your life backs up your message.

Chapter 9

FOLLOW-UP

They drummed it into me. Man alive, how they drummed it into me! When you lead someone to Christ, you are responsible to do all you can to help that new babe in Christ to grow into a mature, dedicated, fruitful disciple of Christ. Recently I received a letter that illustrates this concept.

Roger was seven years old when he smoked marijuana for the first time. By the age of sixteen he was into alcohol, cocaine, crack, LSD, magic mushrooms, and a variety of other drugs. Sin had a tight grip on his life which could be loosened only by the power of God. It was while he was sitting in a jail cell that the Lord finally got through to him, and he turned to Jesus Christ in repentance and faith and received Him as his personal Savior and Lord.

After he was released from jail, he tried to live the Christian life but just couldn't do it. As a result he would struggle with periods of deep depression as he brooded over his failures to live like God wanted him to. One Sunday morning he attended a church where he met Bob who was teaching the college class. He liked what he heard. Bob taught the lessons straight from the Word of God, and

Roger knew that this was what he needed in his life. But when he asked Bob to help him in his walk with the Lord, he didn't realize what he was letting himself in for. Bob wasn't easy on him, but it was just the kind of challenge that Roger needed. Bob helped him begin to memorize Scripture on a regular basis. He also helped him develop the practice of meeting with God in the morning in prayer and Bible reading, before the hustle and bustle of the day.

Roger learned how to study the Bible and, with the help of the Holy Spirit, to apply it to his life. And, he learned to share his faith with others. Through this whole process, Bob was always right there with a word of encouragement. After a few months of this, the Lord brought Monte into Roger's life. Monte and Roger worked in the same store. Roger began to pray for Monte and then had the joy of leading him to Christ. And Roger said, "Now I have the opportunity of helping him just like Bob helped me. Isn't God awesome!"

As I read Bob's letter my heart leaped for joy. Just think of the potential for good and for God that is wrapped up in this little story. It is a modern day example of the ancient truth penned by the Apostle Paul to Timothy, his son in the faith. "And the things that you have heard from me among many witnesses, commit these to faithful men who will be able to teach others also" (2 Timothy 2:2). One of the great truths that shines through this story is the fact that God used Bob to make a difference. Yes, Roger was a believer, but one who was stumbling through life. But the grace of God brought Bob into his life, and Bob helped Roger to get on his feet spiritually and become a man of God who could make a difference himself. In this story, we can see once again the power of the basics that God used to put Roger on the track—things like Scripture memory, Bible study, the quiet time, and witnessing. Oh, I know there is nothing profound in this, but it *is* directly related to the Great Commission of Jesus Christ.

Teaching by Example

The world will not be evangelized by full-time Christian workers alone, but also by people like Roger who reaches out to some guy at work and shares his faith in Christ. And notice, Bob not only taught Roger to witness, but also by example showed him how to teach Monte what Bob had taught him. Let's look at some Scripture passages that bear on this idea.

● We begin with Colossians 1:28-29. "Him we preach, warning every man and teaching every man in all wisdom, that we may present every man perfect in Christ Jesus. To this end I also labor, striving according to His working which works in me mightily." The Apostle Paul had a two-fold ministry of warning and teaching. He was an evangelist, warning people to turn to Christ in repentance and faith and receive Him as their Savior and Lord. The desire of his heart was that he might bring every man up to his full maturity in Christ. He wanted to help those who came to Christ to grow up into the fullness of Christ. "For this I labor (unto weariness) striving with all the superhuman energy which He so mightily inkindles and works within me" (1:29, AMP).

There are some great insights in this passage that show us Paul's philosophy of ministry.

– He is a laborer. He is not afraid of a little hard work. He labors "unto weariness."

– He is a "striver." The word translated striving or struggling is from a Greek word meaning "to agonize." It is often used in connection with athletic events where two runners are striving to break the tape and win the race. They are giving it their all.

– He has superhuman energy. The Word that the Spirit of God led Paul to use here is never used to portray human energy. It is always used to depict superhuman energy—either good or bad but never human. Paul did not labor in the energy of the flesh.

    – This energy is kindled by God's power. And the word he uses to portray God's power is the one from which we get the English word "dynamite." Explosive power. Miraculous power. Great power.

    As we read this passage, we realize that it is not easy to help people in their spiritual growth and bring them to their full maturity in Christ. It is not strolling in the park. But I'm sure Bob would tell you that when Roger came to him with the exciting news of Monte's conversion, it was well worth all his time and effort. And, we must not forget Paul's words in 1 Corinthians 15:10 that bring balance into the picture. "I labored more abundantly than they all, yet not I, but the grace of God which was in me." Paul based it all on the grace of God.

    ● Our second passage that throws light on our study of spiritual growth is also found in Paul's letter to the church in Colosse, Colossians, 2:6-7, "As you have therefore received Christ Jesus the Lord, so walk in Him, rooted and built up in Him and stablished in the faith, as you have been taught, abounding in it with thanksgiving." Here he encourages his grandchildren in the faith to walk in Christ, get their spiritual roots down deep in Christ, become built up in Christ, and become established in the faith.

    What can you and I do to establish new Christians in the faith? Again, Bob, Roger, and Monte are examples to us. We can help new believers become established by teaching them how to maintain a daily fellowship with God through the Word and prayer and to walk with Christ Jesus their Lord by faith. And why does the Apostle Paul encourage this? He gives us one of his reasons in the preceding verses.

That their hearts may be encouraged, being knit together in love, and attaining to all riches of the full assurance of understanding, to the knowledge of the mystery of God, both of the Father and of Christ, in whom are hidden all the treasures of wisdom and knowledge. Now this I say lest anyone should deceive you with persuasive words. For though I am absent in the flesh, yet I am with you in spirit, rejoicing to see your good order, and the steadfastness of your faith in Christ (2:2-5).

Paul speaks of a mighty conflict that rages around him and the spiritual warfare into which these news babes have been thrust. He fears that enticing words will inflict damage of their order and steadfastness. These two words he uses — "order" and "steadfastness" are military terms that carry the picture of an enemy breakthrough of what was once a solid formation of soldiers, something like the U.S. Army experienced at the Battle of the Bulge in Europe, during World War II. So Paul's desire for these new babes is that they might have strong, solid roots from which they can grow and become firmly established in the faith.

I recently saw a picture of the vital need for this. There had been a mighty outpouring of the Spirit of God that brought thousands into Christ's kingdom. Almost immediately false cults and false teachers began to arrive in great numbers in an effort to delude these new Christians with their enticing words. When that sort of thing happened to the young Christians in Paul's ministry he did not give up easily.

He describes his intense battle in Galatians 4:19, "My little children, for whom I labor in birth again until Christ is formed in you." The word *labor* conveys a great pain. He would agonize for them until Christ was formed in them and they were firmly established in the faith.

Guarding New Believers

Lest we get the idea that the Apostle Paul is going a bit overboard in his concept of the danger faced by new babes in Christ, and is overstating the case, see the Apostle Peter's words in 1 Peter 5:8-9, "Be sober, be vigilant; because your adversary the devil walks about like a roaring lion, seeking whom he may devour. Resist him steadfast in the faith, knowing that the same sufferings are experienced by your brotherhood in the world."

Here we look behind the scenes to see who is behind the activities of false teachers, false prophets, and false cults. It is the devil himself, and such a powerful foe needs to be resisted with the powerful weapons of prayer and the Word of God. The prayers of Moses recorded in Exodus 17:11 demonstrate the way the power of God is unleashed on behalf of those in the battle. "And it came to pass, when Moses held up his hand, that Israel prevailed; and when he let down his hand, Amalek prevailed." Joshua was facing a powerful foe, and Moses devoted himself to prayer in his behalf. When Moses prayed, Joshua prevailed over his enemy. But when Moses grew weary and stopped praying for Joshua, the enemy prevailed. This is a clear picture of the need for prayer for those new babes in Christ for whom we carry a responsibility. And, of course, Jesus Himself demonstrated for us the power of the Word of God in defeating the enemy with the words, "It is written."

Some years ago I was in Australia attending a Navigator Staff conference that was being held on a beautiful sheep ranch a few miles from Sydney. One day I was talking to one of the crew working on the sheep ranch, and he told me something about sheep that almost made me ill. It was lambing season on the ranch, and this man told me it was a very dangerous time for the flock. He called my attention to some large birds circling above the place where the mother sheep were kept. He said that quite often one of these large birds would land on the back of the mother sheep and stay there until the baby lamb was born. At that moment the bird would jump down from the back of the mother sheep and eat the tongue and the eyes of the newborn lamb.

As I said, the very idea of such a thing happening almost made me sick. Later on it occurred to me that the devil is like that. Just as the bird went for the eyes and the tongue, so the devil does everything within his power to keep the new convert from developing real insight into the things of Christ and from gaining a vision for the world and its spiritual need, and thus from becoming an outspoken witness for the Savior.

Releasing the Power

The Apostle John paints for us a picture of spiritual growth in 1 John 2:12-14.

> I write to you, little children, because your sins are forgiven you for His name's sake. I write to you, fathers, because you have known Him who is from the beginning. I write to you, young men, because you have overcome the wicked one. I write to you, little children, because you have known the Father. I have written to you, fathers, because you have known Him who is from the beginning. I have written to you, young men, because you are strong, and the Word of God abides in you, and you have overcome the wicked one.

The group that we will look at closely is the young men, the people who have begun to develop some spiritual muscle. They are strong and in their battles with the devil have come out victorious. Now think with me for a moment.

Isn't that what Bob wanted for Roger? I'm sure his heart's desire was to see Roger go through life as a victorious Christian. And I'm equally sure that's what Roger wanted for Monte. But how? Does the Apostle John give us a clue as to the means whereby these young men would become strong overcomers? Yes, of course, he does. In verse 14 where he speaks of strength and victory he says, "the Word of God abides in you." There's the secret! These young men had saturated their hearts and lives with the Word of God and were beginning to experience its power. The Word translated "abides" is from a verb that means to take up residence in a place. These people lived in the Word and the Word lived in them, and the result was strength and victory in their battles with the world, the flesh, and the devil.

The Apostle Paul strikes this same theme in his letter to the church in Thessalonica. "For this reason we also thank God without ceasing, because when you received the Word of God which you heard from us, you welcomed it not as the word of men, but as it is in truth, the Word of God, also effectively works in you who believe" (1 Thessalonians 2:13). The Word of God is set in operation like a huge dynamo in those who believe, exercising its superhuman power. Do you want those whom you lead to Christ to go on to become strong overcomers? If so, do everything in your power to get the Word of God into their lives.

There are two passages of Scripture, one by Paul and the other by John, that are a bit frightening. Paul wrote, "Do all things without murmuring and disputing, that you may become blameless and harmless, children of God without fault in the midst of a crooked and perverse generation, among whom you shine as lights in the world, holding fast the Word of life, that I may rejoice in the day of Christ that I have not run in vain or labored in vain" (Philippians 2:14-16).

Was he saying that unless these people progressed in their spiritual lives to the place where *they* could hold forth the Word of life to others, that Paul looked upon his ministry as having been in vain? It seems to me that is *exactly* what he was saying. But how could that be? These people had become Christians, were in the church, were on their way to heaven! But Paul longed for his ministry to be deeper than that. His dream was to see every member of the body of Christ actively involved in the ministry of the Word to others, just as we saw in Roger and Monte.

Let me ask you a question. How do you see the church? Is it like a huge luxury liner where hundreds of passengers lounge around in deck chairs taking it easy while the crew does the work? Or do you see the church as a rowing team, each person with his oar in the water rowing in unison with the rest of the team striving to win the prize. That's the way the Apostle Paul envisioned the church, and unless every man had his oar in the water and was giving it his all, Paul considered his ministry to be in vain.

The other passage that carries a very serious note is found in 1 John 2:28, "And now, little children, abide in Him; that when He appears, we may have confidence, and not be ashamed before Him at His coming." Does that mean that unless these people were living the abiding life, the Apostle John would be ashamed when he once again saw Christ face-to-face? John took to heart the words of his Lord who said, "Abide in Me, and I in you. As the branch cannot bear fruit of itself, unless it abides in the vine, neither can you, unless you abide in Me. I am the vine, you are the branches. He who abides in Me, and I in him, bears much fruit; for without Me you can do nothing" (John 15:4-5).

Being God's Someone

You may be thinking that all this emphasis on helping Christians in their spiritual growth is not necessary. Aren't they God's children? Surely He is able to take care of His own. Therefore, it would make sense to do what we can to win them to Christ and then give them over to God and let Him care for them. But the Apostle Paul would have an answer to that idea. In Acts 20:31-32, he reminded the Ephesian elders of the fact that for three years he ministered to them night and day with tears. He then said, "And *now*, brethren—*now* after three years of intensive heartfelt ministry, *now* I commend you to God and to the Word of His grace"—but not before. No, the Apostle Paul considered the ministry of follow-up as valid as the ministry of evangelism. Remember, he was both a warner and a teacher.

An interesting pattern of ministry grows out of Acts 16:5. "So the churches were strengthened in the faith, and increased in number daily." The church was established in the faith and grew in attendance. As the individual believers were deepened in their walk with God, they became effective witnesses for Christ. A modern-day example of the strategy comes out of the experience of a church in the British Isles. A young man was called to pastor a church in a town that was known for four things: drunkenness, wife beating, drugs, and child abuse. The church was down to about thirty members and was slowly dying. He began by preaching the Gospel. When people were saved, he helped them become established in the faith. A few years passed and I was invited to minister there for a week. I found a church with 300 active members with each person either discipling someone or being discipled. Today it is a lively, growing church with a strong outreach in the community. One man with a vision of being both a warner and a teacher made the difference.

If there is one thing I hope has been communicated in this chapter it is that follow-up—helping Christians in their spiritual growth—is best done by some*one* and not by some-

thing. It is not a matter of just exposing people to some sort of discipleship program. There are many programs today and most of them are good. But they need to be supplemented with the personal touch of a concerned, caring individual. Paul set the tone when he said, "But we were gentle among you, just as a nursing mother cherishes her own children. So, affectionately longing for you, we were well pleased to impart to you not only the Gospel of God, but also our own lives, because you had become dear to us. . . . You know how we exhorted, and comforted, and charged every one of you, as a father does his own children, that you would have a walk worthy of God, who calls you into His own kingdom and glory" (1 Thessalonians 2:7-8, 11-12).

Some years ago my wife and I moved into a new home. We laid sod and it was such a beautiful lawn that our neighbor decided to call the sod company and have them do the same with his yard. He also put in a sprinkler system. I didn't have the money to put in an automatic sprinkler system, so I bought a long garden hose for my wife to use as she cared for the lawn. His automatic system began to develop problems. Sand plugged up the sprinklers, and it wasn't long before much of his lawn began to dry up and die. By way of contrast, in the evening Virginia would give our lawn her individual, personal attention. Our lawn flourished while our neighbor's lawn died. Follow-up, helping new Christians grow, is best done by some*one,* not some*thing.*

God's plan revolves around people, not programs. Here are six things you can do to help new believers get their feet on solid ground.

• Pray for them. The prayers of Paul provide a guide.

• Don't give up. Spiritual growth has its ups and downs.

● Be a role model. The Corinthians became followers of Paul *and* of the Lord.

● Go slowly. Don't try to accomplish too much too quickly with too many people.

● Practice what you preach. God does not use a lie to teach the truth.

● Keep your spiritual fellowship Bible-based and Christ-centered.

Chapter 10

THE LORDSHIP OF CHRIST

In any discussion of the lordship of Jesus Christ, two factors must always be considered. The one is *objective* — Jesus Christ is Lord. In his powerful message to Cornelius, the Roman military commander who was seeking God, Peter began with a declaration of the lordship of Jesus Christ. He clarified the central issue: "Jesus Christ is Lord of all." And as you and I read those words, we wonder just what "all" includes. For a partial answer to that question, we look at an incident recorded in Mark.

> That day when evening came, He said to His disciples, "Let us go over to the other side." Leaving the crowd behind, they took Him along, just as He was, in the boat. There were also other boats with Him. A furious squall came up, and the waves broke over the boat, so that it was nearly swamped. Jesus was in the stern, sleeping on a cushion. The disciples woke Him and said to Him, "Teacher, don't You care if we drown?" He got up, rebuked the wind, and said to the waves, "Quiet! Be still!" Then the wind died down, and it was completely calm. He said to His disciples, "Why are

you so afraid? Do you still have no faith?" They were
terrified and asked each other, "Who is this? Even the
wind and the waves obey Him!" (4:35-41, NIV)

A second incident is recorded in Mark 5:1-24. Upon
reaching the other side of the lake they were met by a man
under the control of the devil who lived among the tombs;
no one was strong enough to subdue him. When Jesus met
the man, He asked him his name. The man answered, "My
name is Legion; for we are many." Bible scholars tell us that
a Roman legion numbers between 6,000 to 10,000 men.
Here then was a man under the domination of some 6,000
or more demons from hell, and yet, with a Word, the Lord
Jesus dispatched the lot of them and the man was set free.
When Jesus and His men went back across the lake,
they were met by another man with a big problem. Jairus, a
ruler of the synagogue, had a twelve-year-old daughter who
was at the point of death. I have tried to imagine the excitement and gratitude and hope that filled the father's heart
when Jesus agreed to go with him. But no sooner had they
gotten under way than an unexpected delay presents itself.

Now a certain woman had a flow of blood for twelve
years, and had suffered many things from many physi-
cians. She had spent all that she had, and was no better, but rather grew worse. When she heard about
Jesus, she came behind Him in the crowd and touched
His garment; for she said, "If only I may touch His
clothes, I shall be made well." Immediately the foun-
tain of her blood was dried up, and she felt in her body
that she was healed of the affliction. And Jesus, immediately knowing in Himself that power had gone out of
Him, turned around in the crowd and said, "Who
touched My clothes?" But His disciples said to Him,
"You see the multitude thronging You, and You say,

"Who touched Me?" And He looked around to see her who had done this thing. But the woman, fearing and trembling, knowing what had happened to her, came and fell down before Him and told Him the whole truth. And He said to her, "Daughter, your faith has made you well. Go in peace, and be healed of your affliction" (Mark 5:25-34).

I have often tried to put myself in Jairus' shoes. Any delay could be deadly. Remember, the little girl was not just sick — she was at the point of death. And the longer they stood there, the greater the likelihood they would not arrive in time. Jairus was measuring time by heartbeats. And still Jesus stood there listening, as the woman came and fell down before Him and told Him the whole truth. How long do you think that took? Finally the woman's problem was taken care of and they could move on, and then it happened. "While He was still speaking, some came from the ruler of the synagogue's house who said, "Your daughter is dead. Why trouble the teacher any further?" (Mark 5:35) Jairus' hopes were dashed, but Jesus tried to encourage him not to lose heart or faith. And for good reason. When they arrived at the home of Jairus, Jesus took the girl by the hand and she arose from the dead. One of the men who watched all of these remarkable things happen was Peter. He watched as Jesus exercised authority over the wind and the wave. He watched as Jesus healed the sick and raised the dead. So it is no wonder that when He spoke to Cornelius, Peter told him Jesus Christ is Lord of all! (Acts 10:36)

Is He My Lord?

And as you and I read the Bible, we come to the same obvious conclusion. The simple objective fact is that Jesus

Christ is Lord. But then we come to the *subjective* factor. Yes, He is Lord, but is He *my* Lord? Have I submitted my heart, mind, and will to His lordship over my life? We are challenged by the words of the Apostle Paul, "For the love of Christ constrains us, because we judge thus: that if One died for all, then all died; and He died for all, that those who live should live no longer for themselves, but for Him who died for them and rose again" (2 Corinthians 5:14-15).

To make Jesus the Lord of my life means that I no longer live for self but for Him. I seek first the kingdom of God (Matthew 6:33). I set my affections on things above, not on things on the earth (Colossians 3:2). Why must I do this? Jesus gave us the answer, "No one can serve two masters; for either he will hate the one and love the other, or else he will be loyal to the one and despise the other. You cannot serve God and mammon" (Matthew 6:24). I must make a choice. If my destination is self-gratification, self-glory, and self-advancement, I will take one path. But if my desire is to glorify Christ and live under His Lordship, the path I take will lead in a totally different direction.

Another strong reason for making Christ the Lord of my life has to do with ownership. How is ownership defined? By a person being able to say, "That is mine." Let's say I am driving down the street with an architect who points out a house on a hillside and says, "LeRoy, do you see that house up there? That is one of mine." Chuck means, of course, that that house is his own personal design. The next day I am riding down that same street with a builder friend of mine who points to that same house and says, "LeRoy, do you see that house up there? That is one of mine. I built that house." The next day I am going down that same street with a man who buys houses and makes them available for people to rent. He points to that same house and says, "LeRoy, do you see that house up there? That's one of mine. I bought it as a rental property and we hope to make lots of money with that house." The next day I am walking down the street in front of that house when a twelve-year-old boy says hi to me from the front porch. "How do you like my new house, mister?" "Is that your house?" I ask. "Yes," he replies, "my mom and dad and baby sister and I moved in yesterday. I sure do like my new house." Now let me ask you a question. Who is right? Well, of course, they are all right.

In a similar fashion, God has a clear claim on our lives. He designed us; He was the architect. Genesis 1:27 says, "So God created man in His own image; in the image of God He created him; male and female He created them." Also He made us. "Know that the Lord, He is God; it is He who has made us, and not we ourselves; we are His people and the sheep of His pasture" (Psalm 100:3). He has bought us with His own blood, and just like the little boy whose family had moved into their new house, He lives in us. "To them God willed to make known what are the riches of the glory of this mystery among the Gentiles: which is Christ in you, the hope of glory" (Colossians 1:27). So by every criteria, we belong to the Lord. He designed us, He made us, He bought us, and He lives in us. We are His. And that means we must not presume to use for self that which belongs to someone else. People are brought to trial for doing that. For instance, let's say a bank teller is a compulsive gambler. Every so often he takes a few days off from his job at the bank and goes to a gambling resort. He loses his money and in desperation signs a few IOUs and returns to his job. But soon the people who hold his IOUs begin to put the pressure on him to pay up. So he uses some of the bank's money to pay his debt. He tries to cover up his act but is soon discovered and eventually sent to jail. What is his crime? He has tried to use for self that which belonged to someone else.

A few years ago my wife and I were on a preaching

tour throughout Europe. My summer Bible study project was to do an inductive study of the Gospel of Mark. Toward the end of the trip we were at a training program near Helsinki for college students from Finland. One afternoon we were in a small cabin located on an island in the Baltic Sea. My wife was writing some postcards and I was studying Mark 15 when all of a sudden a scriptural truth practically leaped off the pages of the Bible. "Right," I exclaimed, "That's right!" My wife was startled. "What's right?" she asked. The passage was Mark 15:31, "Likewise, the chief priests together with the scribes mocked and said among themselves, 'He saved others; Himself He cannot save.' "

As the chief priests and scribes mocked the Lord Jesus, they unknowingly hit upon a deep spiritual truth: If you want to be used by God to save others, you cannot hold on to your own life and use it for yourself. You cannot take your life, put it into a safety deposit box, and keep it hidden away and used for your own pleasures. A life lived for Christ will be dedicated to Him.

When we left Helsinki we went to Sweden to minister the Word at a week-long deeper life conference. While we were there, we met a girl named Ruth who told us a fascinating story. On New Year's Eve she joined with other members of her church to pray in the New Year. Like many congregations around the world, it was their practice to greet the New Year on their knees in prayer to the Lord. The minister suggested that during their individual prayer time each member of the church pray over Paul's comments to the church in Rome which emphasizes the admonition that they present their bodies as a living sacrifice to the Lord and in that way totally give themselves to God (Romans 12:1). Ruth did that and one by one gave her eyes and ears and voice and arms and legs and hands and feet to Christ. When the prayer time ended, Ruth left for home. As she was walking, the driver of a huge bus lost control on the icy street; the bus jumped the curb, ran into Ruth, and sent her flying through the air. She awakened in the hospital and discovered that in order to save her life, the doctors had to amputate her right leg. When the members of the church heard what had happened, they came by to express their sorrow. But Ruth did not need consolation. She told those who came to see her that on New Year's Eve she had given her body to the Lord and whatever He wanted to do with her legs or hands or eyes or voice was up to Him. And then she made this remarkable statement, "You cannot lose what you have given away."

Are You Wasting Your Life?

Some months ago I had a rather sad conversation with a friend of mine. He said, "LeRoy, I think I have wasted my life. For fifty years I have worked hard and given my life to my business, but as I look back over those years, it is clear to me that my life has not been lived for the Lord but for my own welfare, pleasure, and comfort." And then he made this heartbreaking statement. "LeRoy," he said, "I'd give anything if I could live those years over. I'd give anything if I could buy those years back." But, of course, he could not do that. There is not enough money in the world for him to be able to buy back those years. And that is what Jesus was getting at when He asked the question, "Or what would you give to buy back your life?"

Dr. Howard Hendricks told of a man who came to him with this same problem. The man said, "Howie, years ago I put my ladder up against the wall and began to climb. For all these years since then I have struggled to make it to the top. Now I've arrived only to discover that fifty years ago I placed my ladder against the wrong wall."

One summer a young pastor came to Glen Eyrie and at

the beginning of his third sermon gave us a little quiz to see if we were alert. He told us of a bus that rolled into town with twenty passengers. At the bus stop thirteen people got off and seven got on. At the next stop three got off and nineteen got on. At the next stop twelve got on and eighteen got off. At the last stop ten got on and three got off. Then he said, "Now here is the obvious question. How many stops did the bus make?" After the laughter subsided he said, "For the last seventy seconds we have done what millions spend seventy years doing—trying to find the answer to the wrong question. How can I get rich? How can I live a life of pleasure? How can I become famous? And all the while the words of Jesus are ignored. "For whoever desires to save his life will lose it, but whoever loses his life for My sake and the Gospel's will save it" (Mark 8:35). There are a number of very good reasons for living my life under the lordship of Jesus Christ.

● One is found in James 4:14, "You do not know what will happen tomorrow. For what is your life? It is even a vapor that appears for a little time and then vanishes away." Life is too short to be little. Don't allow yourself to settle for a tiny little life. The next time you are where the temperature is low enough for you to see your breath, do this. Step outside and blow your breath into the air. Then, as you watch your breath appear and then vanish away, say to yourself, "That is my life." And make sure you only blow once. If you blow twice, you have just doubled your life span and you can't do that. You can do it only once. Your life is just *one* vapor.

● Another good reason for denying self and living under Christ's Lordship is found in 2 Peter 3:10, "But the day of the Lord will come as a thief in the night, in which the heavens will pass away with a great noise, and the elements will melt with fervent heat; both the earth and the works that are in it will be burned up." Give your life to something that will last. Set your affections on things above, not on the things of this earth. And the only things that will last for all eternity are God, His Word, and the souls of people. Everything you see is going to burn.

I was discussing this with a friend of mine who lives in Hong Kong. He was telling me about his brother who is all caught up in the mad Hong Kong scramble to make money. He is investing, buying real estate, and working sixteen hours a day. He has no time for God at all. His life revolves around the accumulation of things, a bigger and bigger bank account, and safety deposit boxes stuffed with stocks and bonds. I asked him how he felt about his brother's lifestyle. He said it makes him sad, because when this life ends, his brother will have at his side a large pile of smoldering ashes. It's all going to burn.

• A third reason for making Christ the Lord of my life is found in 1 Corinthians 15:58, "Therefore, my beloved brethren, be steadfast, unmovable, always abounding in the work of the Lord, knowing that your labor is not in vain in the Lord." Whatever you do in the name of Christ and for His sake counts for something. It matters.

Some years ago I read the history of a very costly battle that was fought in the Pacific during World War II. After years of reflection, it was determined by military strategists that the battle should never have been fought. The Allies should have circumvented the island and simply ignored it until the end of the war. It would have saved the lives of hundreds of young Japanese soldiers and American military personnel. The battle was fought, and the Allies won the battle, but it was all in vain. However, if you live your life for the sake of Christ and for His glory under His lordship, there will never be placed on the pages of your life "This life was lived in vain." But that will be the recurring theme of a life lived for self.

What does it mean then to deny self? The word *deny* means to "refuse association with," to "have no companionship with, to repudiate." When Peter denied Christ, he refused to admit that he had any association with Him; He repudiated his companionship with the Lord. And it is interesting to note that you can do that only with someone you know. You wouldn't go up to a total stranger and say, "You and I are through. I'm going to stop associating with you." Our problem is that we know self very well. We go back a long ways. But when we come to the place where we desire to repudiate self, that self will argue and object. It will whine and whimper, "We've had such a good time together. Think of the good old days." Self will argue and plead. But the call of Jesus Christ on our lives to live under His Lordship is an exclusive one. We have to choose. We cannot serve self when it is the easy thing to do, and then serve Christ when it is convenient. There must be a definite break with the self-life.

Which Direction Will You Take?

As we close this chapter, let me ask you a question. Have you ever placed your life on the altar of God to be consumed in the fires of His love? You can do that right now. Visualize in your mind's eye a group of people all facing one direction. You are all looking at one person, the Lord Jesus Christ, and He is looking at you. It is dusk. Finally He speaks, "If anyone desires to come after Me, let him deny himself, and take up his cross daily, and follow Me" (Luke 9:23). He then turns and begins to walk slowly away. At that moment, what do you see yourself doing? Do you see yourself stepping out from the crowd and following the Lord?

Or do you see yourself turning around, pushing your way through the crowd, and going off into the darkness? To turn your back on the Lord is to guarantee disaster. You will have no firm foundation upon which you can build your life. You will be like the man Jesus told of, who "built his house upon the earth without a foundation; against which the stream beat vehemently, and immediately it fell. And the ruin of that house was great (Luke 6:49).

Here then are four questions to help you determine who is Lord of your life.

• How do you spend your time? In selfish pleasure or in seeking first the kingdom of God?

• Do you see your life as a personal possession or belonging to the Lord?

• What do your check stubs reveal? Do you use your money for selfish pleasure or to advance the cause of Christ?

• In the gray areas of questionable activities do you try to see how much you can get away with without incurring the wrath of God?

Remember the words of Jesus: "And why do you call Me 'Lord,' and do not the things which I say?" (Luke 6:46)

Chapter 11

OBEDIENCE

Obedience is not automatic. A lifestyle of obedience to the Word of God begins with a deep commitment. And one of the clearest passages in Scripture that brings out this point is found in the writings of the Apostle Peter, "Therefore gird up the loins of your mind, be sober, and rest your hope fully upon the grace that is to be brought to you at the revelation of Jesus Christ; as obedient children, not conforming yourselves to the former lusts, as in your ignorance; but as He who called you is holy, you also be holy in all your conduct, because it is written, 'Be holy, for I am holy!' " (1 Peter 1:13-16)

God's grand design for His people is twofold. First, that we live a lifestyle of obedience and second, that we may take on more and more of His likeness day by day. "But we all, with unveiled face, beholding as in a mirror the glory of the Lord, are being transformed into the same image from glory to glory, just as by the Spirit of the Lord" (2 Corinthians 3:18).

In order to do this, we must gird up the loins of our minds. Now I realize that sounds a bit strange to our ears, but to the people of the Middle East who wore long flowing robes, it made perfect sense. If you saw a man heading down the road with his long flowing robe hiked up under his belt, you knew he was not out for a leisurely stroll. To gird up the loins of the mind indicates you mean business; it is like taking off your coat and rolling up your sleeves. You are getting ready for a tough task. It is not the picture of a slow drive through the countryside, but of an ambulance heading for the emergency room.

But not only must you live a surrendered life but also a focused life. There are distractions of every kind that call us to leave the path of obedience and expend our energies looking for an easier road, a smoother road, a broader road. Peter tells us that it would be a disgraceful thing for people whose motive is obedience to turn around and go back to the sins of a former time. Nevertheless, those allurements are there, so we must fix our minds on the paths of obedience and keep them there.

When I was living on my brother's farm in Southwest Iowa, it would often be my task to cultivate the corn. We had two teams of horses Molly and Bess, and Bud and Nance. Molly and Bess were older and knew exactly what was expected of them. If we started them down the corn row, they stayed in it. Bud and Nance, however, were easily distracted. They had a tendency to gaze around the field and meander off the path. For that reason we put blinders on them to keep them focused in the right direction. A deep, bedrock commitment to a lifestyle of obedience has the same effect. It is something the Spirit of God can use to help us press toward the mark. Obedience is not automatic.

Holy Obedience

The Apostle Peter goes on to call us to a life of holiness — a life that is set apart for God's service. And a holy life finds its example in God Himself. The children of disobedience we find in Ephesians 2:2 have now been transformed by the Spirit of God into children of obedience who reproduce the family lifestyle of holiness.

To live as a Christian does not mean merely accepting a system of doctrine as true. No, to live as a Christian is to experience the controlling power of God in your life on a day-by-day basis. Paul taught that "the kingdom of God is not in word but in power" (1 Corinthians 4:20). When God reaches into the hearts of people, they experience the divine power of His love, mercy, and grace. When you truly experience His saving power, you respond with true faith, true repentance, and true love.

Over the years I have had an ongoing conversation with a young man who knows all the right words. He can clearly articulate the Gospel message and has a verse of Scripture to fit almost any situation. The problem is that he has never experienced the controlling power of God in his life. His fine words are just that—words. There is no reality in what he says. Somewhere along the line he was led to believe that if you could articulate the facts, that was the end of it. Obedience has never played an important role in his life. But Jesus taught, "If you *know* these things, happy are you if you *do* them" (John 13:17). Knowledge plus obedience must accompany us on our daily path if we want to live a life of victory and fruitfulness in His service.

The Results of Obedience

What should be the result of hearing the Word preached? In James 1:22 we are told, "Be doers of the Word, and not hearers only, deceiving yourselves." To be a hearer and not a doer is a form of self-deception. Jesus spelled out for us the way to a happy life that is lived under the blessing of

God, "Blessed are they that hear the Word of God and keep it." Obedience should be the outcome of hearing the Word preached.

What should be the result of Bible reading? An interesting answer to this question is spelled out for us in the life of the Old Testament people of God. They had returned to Jerusalem from their captivity and one of the first things they did in assembly was to have a public reading of the Word. "So they read distinctly from the book, in the law of God; and they gave the sense, and helped them to understand the reading" (Nehemiah 8:8). Later in that chapter a heartwarming scene occurs, where the people discover "that the Children of Israel should dwell in booths during the feast of the seventh month" (v. 14). What was their response? Instant obedience. "The people went out and . . . made themselves booths" (v. 16). Now I know that does not sound like much of a big deal. But think with me for a moment. What if everyone in your church responded with instant and joyful obedience when they read the Word or when the Word was read during the Sunday morning service? That's what these people did. Yes, the result of reading the Word should be obedience.

What should be the result of Bible study? Proverbs 2:1-5 gives us guidance. "My son, if you receive my words, and treasure my commands within you, so that you incline your ear unto wisdom, and apply your heart to understanding; yes, if you cry out for discernment, and lift up your voice for understanding, if you seek her as silver, and search for her as for hidden treasures; then you will understand the fear of the Lord, and find the knowledge of God." And the outcome of seeking and searching and heartfelt prayer is given in verse 20—"So you may walk in the way of goodness and keep the paths of righteousness." Once again we see the importance God places on obedience to His Word.

What should be the result of Scripture memory? "But

the word is very near you, in your mouth and in your heart,
that you may do it" (Deuteronomy 30:14). I have a friend
who came to Christ while he was in the Armed Forces. The
Christian guys began to talk to him about memorizing the
Word. He was eager to grow so they helped him get started.
He had a remarkable mind and an insatiable hunger for the
Word that resulted in his memorizing hundreds of verses
the first year. It also resulted in a bad case of pride. He had
a verse for everything. When a friend began a weightlifting
program he told him, "Bodily exercise profiteth little." If
someone missed his quiet time, my friend was right there
with, "He that is faithful in that which is least is faithful also
in much." If one of the Christian guys enjoyed singing along
when the Sons of the Pioneers sang the old western ballad
"Cool Water," my friend had a verse for him. "Are any of
you merry? Let him sing psalms." His Scripture memory
resulted in pride and in his making a nuisance of himself.
But the Bible says the result should be obedience.

The Necessity of Obedience

A life of obedience is necessary if we are to enjoy other
aspects of the Christian life.

• Obedience is necessary if we want to have close fellowship with God. The Apostle John says, "This is the message
which we have heard from Him, and declare to you, that
God is light and in Him is no darkness at all. If we say that
we have fellowship with Him, and walk in darkness, we lie
and do not practice the truth. But if we walk in the light as
He is in the light, we have fellowship one with another, and
the blood of Jesus Christ His Son cleanses us from all sin"
(1 John 1:5-7). Our lives should reflect the Light of the
World. But walking in God's light reveals our sins and

shortcomings and thus we see our need for cleansing through the blood of Jesus Christ His Son who cleanses us from all sin. If we think we can live in the dark, and at the same time have fellowship with the One in whom is no darkness at all, we deceive ourselves.

The Apostle Paul asked five questions of the Corinthians. "Do not be unequally yoked together with unbelievers. For what fellowship has righteousness with lawlessness? And what communion has light with darkness? And what accord has Christ with Belial? Or what part has a believer with an unbeliever? And what agreement has the temple of God with idols? For you are the temple of the living God. As God has said, 'I will dwell in them and walk among them. I will be their God, and they shall be My people' " (2 Corinthians 6:14-16). Sin always erects a barricade to try to keep us from close, intimate fellowship with God.

● Obedience is necessary for an effective prayer life. The Apostle John tells us, "And whatever we ask we receive from Him, because we keep His commandments and do those things that are pleasing in His sight" (1 John 3:22). It seems to me that this verse explains the barrenness and the weakness of many prayer lives. Answered prayer is tied firmly to obedience. The promise made in 1 John 3:22 must, of course, be looked upon in the light of other portions of Scripture where God promises to hear and answer the prayers of His people. First John 5:14-15 is one of those: "Now this is the confidence that we have in Him, that if we ask any thing according to His will, He hears us. And if we know that He hears us, whatever we ask, we know that we have the petitions that we have asked of Him." It seems to me that those who live in obedience to the will of God and keep His commandments are simply demonstrating that their wills are in sync with God and their prayers reflect that fact.

• Obedience is necessary if we want to be good witnesses for our Lord. First Corinthians 15:34 says, "Awake to righteousness, and do not sin; for some do not have the knowledge of God. I speak this to your shame." Our lives must stack up to what we say. Also note 1 Thessalonians 1:5, "For our Gospel did not come to you in word only, but also in power, and in the Holy Spirit, and in much assurance, as you know what kind of men we were among you for your sake." The apostles practiced what they preached. Your life can either weaken the message or reinforce it. The people God used to bring my wife and me to Christ lived a life of obedience and dedication to the Lord. We were attracted by their lives, and their witness was used of God to bring us to Christ.

• Obedience is necessary if we are to abide in Christ's love. The words of Jesus in John 15:10 bear this out. "If you keep My commandments, you will abide in My love, just as I have kept My Father's commandments, and abide in His love." To abide in His love we must live lives of obedience. When Jesus speaks of abiding in His love, He is not attempting to lead us off into some ecstatic, spiritual rapture. It is simply a call to obedience. And in the next verse Jesus makes it clear that He is not trying to lead His followers into some joyless, barren lifestyle. Joy comes when we are totally committed to a life of obedience. "These things I have spoken to you, that My joy may remain in you, and that your joy may be full" (v. 11).

• Obedience demonstrates our love for Christ. "He who has My commandments and keeps them it is he who loves Me. And he who loves Me will be loved by My Father, and I will love him and manifest Myself to him" (John 14:21). In our songs we can *declare* our love for Jesus. In our prayers we can *declare* our love for Jesus. But it is through obedience that we *demonstrate* our love for Jesus. Remember, when we are born again into the kingdom of God, we have a King, a Lord. So what we are called upon to do is to find out what our King wants and then go and do that.

• Our obedience to the Lord is a primary means of helping younger Christians grow and develop in their Christian life. We are to set the pace for those who are new in the faith. Paul wrote, "The things which you learned and received and heard and saw in me, these do, and the God of peace will be with you" (Philippians 4:9). Paul's training of the church at Philippi was not only through his words but through his life. Even Jesus Himself did not rely on words alone in His training of the Twelve. The Bible tells us that no one ever spoke like Jesus, and yet even He did not say, "Listen to Me," but "Follow Me" (Matthew 4:19).

• A life of obedience can do much to silence the enemies of the Cross. Notice Peter's words in 1 Peter 2:15, "For this is the will of God, that by doing good you may put to silence the ignorance of foolish men." These people are put to silence not by our arguing well, but by living well, by *doing* well. God often uses a godly life to attract people to the Savior. Admittedly, faith does not come by seeing, but by hearing. There must be that verbal witness. But the path to a verbal witness for Christ is often via a life that is lived in obedience to the will of God.

• A life of obedience brings glory to God. "Let your light so shine before men, that they may see your good works and glorify your Father in heaven" (Matthew 5:16). This brings obedience to a place of remarkable importance. The reason? Because the Lord has created us for His glory (Isaiah 43:7). Man's chief purpose for being on this earth is to glorify God. And one of the primary means of bringing honor and glory to God is to live a life of obedience to the will of God.

● A life of obedience evidences the fact that we truly know the Lord. The Apostle Paul pointed out this truth to Titus when he wrote, "They profess to know God, but in works they deny Him, being abominable, disobedient, and disqualified for every good work" (Titus 1:16). They can talk all they want to, but their disobedient lives deny what they say. The Apostle John has some mighty strong words on this point. "Now by this we know that we know Him, if we keep His commandments. He who says, 'I know Him,' and does not keep His commandments, is a liar, and the truth is not in him. But whoever keeps His word, truly the love of God is perfected in him. By this we know that we are in Him" (1 John 2:3-5).

● Obedience is the way to a happy, abundant, blessed life. James tells us, "For if anyone is a hearer of the Word and not a doer, he is like a man observing his natural face in a mirror; for he observes himself, goes away, and immediately forgets what kind of man he was. But he who looks into the perfect law of liberty and continues in it, and is not a forgetful hearer but a doer of the work, this one will be blessed in what he does." Did you happen to notice something strange in that passage? The Bible is called "the perfect law of liberty."

Now, I don't normally associate law with liberty. Law is more often associated with restraints than with freedom and liberty. When I am driving down the freeway and I see a highway patrol car, I automatically slow down no matter how fast or how slow I am traveling; my immediate reaction is to reduce my speed. Law and liberty do not seem to go hand in hand, but James says they do. In what way?

The train that jumps the track does not find liberty. Its

so-called freedom has brought destruction and pain. When I was an employee of the Chicago Great Western Railroad, an old-timer told me that the rules governing the movement of trains were written in blood. In the past someone had done something that caused a train wreck, so they wrote a rule to try to insure that it would not happen again. The law of liberty was not given to restrict you but to lead you into the happy, abundant life.

I'm sure you know people who radiate the presence of the Lord. When you are with them you feel you are close to God. Shortly before his death at the age of ninety-six, my wife and I had the privilege of visiting Dr. Herbert Lockyer in his home. It was like being in the presence of the Lord Himself. This man had walked in fellowship with and obedience to the Lord Jesus for decades. The promise of Jesus had come true — "he who has My commandments and keeps them . . . I will love him and manifest Myself to him" (John 14:21). What greater joy could there be than to have our Lord Jesus reveal more and more of Himself to us. Moses reminded the people that if they would live in obedience to the Word of God, "The glory of the Lord will appear unto you" (Leviticus 9:6).

As we bring this chapter on obedience to a close, let me call your attention to Deuteronomy 30:19-20,

I call heaven and earth as witnesses today against you, that I have set before you life and death, blessing and cursing: therefore choose life, that both you and your descendants may live; that you may love the Lord your God, that you may obey His voice, and that you may cling to Him, for He is your life and the length of your days; and that you may dwell in the land which the Lord swore to your fathers, to Abraham, Isaac, and Jacob, to give them.

To learn the Word of God and then not obey the Word of God is to learn it in vain. Here are four questions to evaluate your obedience.

- Is it total or partial?

- Is it immediate?

- Is it joyful?

- Is it prompted by the right motives?

Chapter 12

THE HOLY SPIRIT

At a Young Life meeting years ago, I heard about a conversation between two cows. They were in the pasture and saw a milk truck pass on a nearby road. Painted on the truck were these words: "Milk: Pasturized, Homogenized, Fortified with Vitamin A, Fortified with Vitamin D." The one cow turned to the other and said, "It makes you feel a bit inadequate, doesn't it?" Well, folks, that's the way I often feel when I open the Word of God. And I suppose I'm not alone. We know in the depths of our souls that we desire to love the Lord our God with all our heart, soul, strength, and mind. And we know that we desire above all else to follow God's leading, do what He wants us to do, and go where He wants us to go. But at the same time, we can be struck with a profound sense of inadequacy. The standards of discipleship can overwhelm us.

These standards have as their base the very character of Christ Himself. You will find yourself crying out with the Apostle Paul, "Who is sufficient for these things?" (2 Corinthians 2:16). Can you and I love as Christ loved? His new commandment to love one another as He loved us seems out of reach (John 13:34). And even if we can love one another, we will be staggered by the Word of Christ, as recorded in Matthew 5:44, "But I say to you, love your enemies, bless those who curse you, do good to those who hate you, and pray for those who despitefully use you and persecute you." And when we read that we are to be imitators of God (Ephesians 5:1), if we are honest we will admit that we can't imitate Chuck Swindoll or Ray Stedman or even the late Bing Crosby. And as we are confronted by these and many other commands in Scripture, we come to the conclusion that they are not only difficult—they are impossible.

Try to imagine the sense of inadequacy the apostles must have felt when Jesus told them they were to make disciples of all nations and preach the Gospel to every creature. After all, they were only eleven very ordinary men, none of whom even *spoke* the language of the Parthians or of the Medes or the people of Mesopotamia. They could not even understand these peoples, let alone evangelize them.

I'm sure their devotion was severely tested, but Jesus had a plan. Yes, they were weak. Yes, they were but a little band. Yes, they still had a long way to go in their character development and their commitment to the mission. But Jesus had no intention of sending them out as they were. He told them, "Behold, I send the Promise of my Father upon you; but tarry in the city of Jerusalem until you are endued with power from on high" (Luke 24:49). When they received that power from on high, they could then launch forth with confidence—not in themselves but in God. Jesus told them, "But you shall receive power when the Holy Spirit has come upon you; and you shall be witnesses to me in Jerusalem, and in all Judea and Samaria, and to the ends of the earth" (Acts 1:8).

Paul summarized it all with these words, "Not that we are sufficient of ourselves to think of anything as being from ourselves, but our sufficiency is from God, who also made us sufficient as ministers of the new covenant, not of the letter but of the Spirit; for the letter kills, but the Spirit gives life" (2 Corinthians 3:5-6). And in his further word to the church at Corinth, Paul painted a graphic picture of the strength and indispensability of inadequacy. He wrote, "But we have this treasure in earthen vessels, that the excellence of the power may be of God and not of us" (2 Corinthians 4:7). His reliance was on the very power of God Himself, a power that speaks of a dynamic, an ability, energy, and capability. So when the Word of God calls us to walk even as Christ walked (1 John 2:6), we do not throw up our hands in despair and cry out that we can't do it. No, we launch out in confidence in His strength. We obey the commands of God by the power of God.

The Power of the Spirit

Over the years Christians around the globe have found comfort in the words of Christ, recorded in John 14:16-17. "And I will pray the Father, and He will give you another Helper, that He may abide with you forever, even the Spirit of truth, whom the world cannot receive, because it neither sees Him nor knows Him; but you know Him, for He dwells with you and will be in you." Here Jesus tells us that this One who will come to us in power will be a Helper and will be with us forever.

The Holy Spirit never answers calls for temporary help. We have in our town a company that furnishes assistance to other companies who need someone to come for a day or a week — possibly even for a month. But the Holy Spirit would not qualify for that kind of position. He never lends assistance for a day or two. Jesus said that this unfailing source of wisdom and strength would not render occasional aid, but would be with us forever. But bear in mind that in order for the Spirit of God to function unhindered in and through our lives, our hearts must be filled with an obedient love for Christ. It was for that reason that Jesus prefaced His remarks about the ministry of the Holy Spirit with these words. "If you love Me, keep My commandments" (John 14:15). And bear in mind also that these men who deeply loved the Lord Jesus, and who knew His departure was near, were not to be abandoned as orphans but were to have another Helper who would take His place. The restraints imposed on Jesus while He was on earth were to be taken away, giving the Holy Spirit free reign to be actively involved in the lives of Christ's followers around the world, transforming their inadequacies into confidence and power. This was driven home to me in an experience I had while in Kota Kinabalu, a city in Sabah, East Malaysia. I was to speak at a conference at 7:30 P.M. It was 7:25 and I was lying in a crumpled heap on the bathroom floor, throwing up everything I had eaten. I was a soggy, perspiring mess, so weak I could hardly move. I called out to my wife, and asked her to contact the emcee and say I couldn't make it to the meeting. Then I remembered that people had been planning and praying for this conference for over a year.

The Lord brought to mind some verses that I had memorized, "You shall receive power" (Acts 1:8), and, "Trust in the Lord with all your heart" (Proverbs 3:5). I began to reconsider. Would God enable me to fulfill the task He had given me? I took courage and asked my wife not to contact the emcee. I staggered to my feet, washed up as best I could, put on a clean shirt, and got my Bible. In minutes we were on our way to the meeting.

When I arrived it was as though I had never had a sick day in my life. I have never experienced a greater sense of God's presence and strength. By all accounts God mightily blessed the meeting. But five minutes after I returned to my hotel room, I was back on the bathroom floor, perspiring and vomiting. If I had not gone to the meeting, the people would have excused me and understood. But God was waiting for me to take a step of faith so He could provide the power I needed.

There is a tremendous power and an abundance of fruitfulness that results when your primary objective in life is in perfect harmony with the primary objective of the Holy Spirit.

The Work of the Spirit

We have been created to glorify the Lord. And, of course, that is the primary goal of the Holy Spirit as well. Jesus told us the Holy Spirit "will not speak on His own authority, but . . . He shall glorify me" (John 16:13-14). I saw an example of this truth some years ago when my wife and I attended an opera at the magnificent opera house in Vienna, Austria. We were seated in the top row of the highest balcony. As the opera progressed I became aware of some activity just behind us. There was a man with a spotlight whose job it was to keep the light focused on the prominent persons on stage. As the singers walked back and forth on the stage, the job of the man behind us was to keep the light on them. As I watched all of this, it occurred to me that that's the way the Holy Spirit works. It is the Spirit's job to keep the light of the Word of God focused on Christ as He performs His ministry around the world. And it would have done a great disservice to the man with the spotlight to ask him to leave his post and go down to the stage and share the spotlight with the central figure of the opera. That was not his place. His place was behind the scenes, in the shadows, calling our attention to the one who was the preeminent person in the story.

And so it is with the Holy Spirit. His desire is to remain in the shadows and make the Lord Jesus Christ, who is the head of the church, the object of our devotion, "that in all things He may have the preeminence" (Colossians 1:18). Yes, we are completely dependent on the Holy Spirit, relying on His power, wisdom, and ability. And the pages of church history are littered with the ruins and wreckage of the lives of people who relied on their own power and wisdom. Recently, I had dinner with a man who was mightily used of God in the lives of scores of young men and women. He taught them the basics of the Christian life and led many of them into lives of fruitfulness and great spiritual usefulness in the kingdom of God. But he had some potential problems that plagued him throughout these years of outstanding service for Christ. One potential problem was his I.Q. He had a brilliant mind and found it easy at times to figure things on his own and leave God out of the picture. Another potential problem was his outstanding speaking ability. He could put messages together and deliver them with such convincing clarity that oftentimes he relied on that ability and left God out of the picture. He had memorized Proverbs 3:5 which says, "Trust in the Lord with all your heart, and lean not on your own understanding," but he abandoned the truth of that verse. He had memorized 2 Samuel 22:33 and could preach on that verse which says, "God is my strength and power, and He makes my way perfect," but he began to trust in his own strength and ability. He became just one more slick professional who thought he could make it on his own. He fell into a variety of sins and was shortly out of the race. He had no interest in laying aside every weight and the sin which entangled him. He got his eyes off the Lord Jesus Christ, the author and perfecter of our faith (Hebrews 12:1), and began to rely on himself. His sufficiency came not from the Holy Spirit but from his own energy and mental powers. Soon his energy ran out and his usefulness to God came to a standstill.

Something like this happened to King Saul. There stood the armies of Israel quaking at the sight of Goliath. Saul looked at Goliath. He knew the command of God to rid the land of the Philistines, but he got his eyes off God and fixed on this nine-foot nine-inch giant. Then he looked around at his men. He looked at himself. He looked at his spear and compared it to the gigantic spear of his enemy. And so there he sat, a man who understood the will of God but not the power of God. And then into the story walks David, the shepherd lad. "And David said to Saul, 'Let no man's heart fail because of him; your servant will go and fight with this Philistine' " (1 Samuel 17:32). He then turned his attention to the giant. "Then said David to the Philistine, 'You come to me with a sword, with a spear, and with a javelin. But I come to you in the name of the Lord of hosts, the God of the armies of Israel, whom you have defied . . . All this assembly shall know that the Lord does not save with sword and spear; for the battle is the Lord's, and He will give you into our hands" (1 Samuel 17:45, 47). What happened after that is known by millions around the world. A youth — totally inadequate for the task — defeated the Philistine through the power of God.

The Filling of the Spirit

It is a wonderful thing to memorize Ephesians 5:18 which tells us to be filled with the Spirit. It is helpful to go to our study books and discover that the command to be filled with the Spirit, is in the present imperative, which means we should be doing it all the time. We understand that we should walk in the Spirit, and that if we do, we will not fulfill the lust of the flesh. But how? How do we live by the power of the Holy Spirit? Let's begin by taking a look at Philippians 2:12-13, "Therefore, my beloved, as you have always obeyed, not as in my presence only, but now much more in my absence, work out your own salvation with fear and trembling; for it is God who works in you both to will and to do for His good pleasure."

• The first step is to realize that the Holy Spirit is already busily at work in you to create in you both the will and the power to do His good pleasure. The work is God's. He does it all. But in His working He puts us to work, although our part is secondary to His. The instant we turn to Christ in repentance and faith, and receive Him into our hearts, He begins His work in us by His Spirit and He never stops. One of His first acts in my life when I came to Christ was to create in me a distaste for my sinful lifestyle. Things that had brought me much pleasure before I came to Christ now left a bitter taste in my heart. Before I came to Christ, I spent every Sunday with a few buddies guzzling beer, smoking cigarettes, and playing poker. After I came to Christ, I stopped all of that and went to church. Before I came to Christ, lewd remarks and blasphemy filled my speech. After I came to Christ, I not only stopped swearing, but I hated it when I heard others take the name of the Lord in vain. God was at work in me. Before I came to Christ, I was a self-centered person. After I came to Christ, I became concerned for others and wanted to learn how to pray for them. Before I came to Christ, the Bible meant nothing to me. After I came to Christ, I had a deep hunger to learn what it taught. And God continued to do His work in me.

Some years after I became a Christian, I was in a filling station getting the car serviced and I stepped inside to get a bottle of pop from the pop machine. I dropped a coin in the machine and out came a Coke. I was elated. Why? Because the sign of the machine gave the price and I had gotten a bottle for half price. For some reason the machine had released the Coke before I had a chance to deposit the second coin. I had beat the machine! But then the Holy Spirit took over. "LeRoy," He said, "what you are doing is not right." "But wait," I pleaded, "surely somewhere in my past a machine has beaten me out of my money and now I am just getting even." "LeRoy," the Holy Spirit answered, "you know that is not your money." So after a brief argument I went to the station attendant and gave him his money. God was at work in me.

● The second step is to realize that He desires to lead you in a new direction. "I say then, 'Walk in the Spirit, and you shall not fulfill the lust of the flesh' " (Galatians 5:16). And then Paul goes on to say that there is a fork in the road up ahead and we must choose our path carefully. He says, "For the flesh lusts against the Spirit, and the Spirit against the flesh; and these are contrary to one another, so that you do not do the things that you wish" (Galatians 5:17). The Spirit wants to take us in one direction and the flesh tries to take us in another. So, step number two is simply a matter of obedience. We are made to understand that we will have to say no to the flesh and yes to the Spirit, because they are going in two different directions. So the obvious conclusion is, "If we live in the Spirit, let us also walk in the Spirit" (Galatians 5:25). The Holy Spirit desires to lead us, and if we are to live by His power and experience His sufficiency, we need to follow where He leads.

Follow the One Up Front

A few years ago my wife and I were asked to go to Semarang, a city of around a million people in North Central Java. I had been asked to teach a ten day course on spiritual leadership to sixty up-and-coming young leaders who assembled from all over Indonesia. The organizers of the seminar arranged for us to stay in a small downtown hotel. As is my custom, the next morning after our arrival, I attempted to get some exercise. I put on my sweats and my athletic shoes and prepared to go for a walk around the downtown area. I went down to the street that led downtown but was afraid to step off the curb. The traffic was horrendous. I had never seen anything like it in my life. Huge trucks came rumbling along at breakneck speed. Taxicabs, motorcycles, and buses, roared through the intersection. And just to add a bit of exotic flavor, there was an ox cart or two. I turned back and got my exercise by walking up and down the hill in front of the hotel. And from time to time I would glance over at the intersection and watch the traffic. The worst were the young men on their huge, loud motorcycles. No, I take that back. The worst were the young ladies sitting side-saddle on the backseat behind the young men. These girls were absolutely unconcerned for their safety. Some were painting their fingernails. Others were reading a book. As I watched them, I asked myself, "How can they be so relaxed? How can they be so unconcerned about their safety? And then it hit me. The only way these young ladies could get through that wild and crazy intersection with such calm assurance was to have absolute confidence in the one up front.

And as I stood there, I saw it as a parable of the Christian life. You and I live in a dangerous world. With Paul, "we are hard-pressed on every side, yet not crushed; we are perplexed, but not in despair; persecuted, but not forsaken; struck down, but not destroyed" (2 Corinthians 4:8-9). We are constantly stalked by "a roaring lion, seeking whom he may devour" (1 Peter 5:8). We are tempted by "the lust of the flesh, the lust of the eyes, and the pride of life" (1 John 2:16). And the only way we can make it through this life is by absolute confidence in the One up front, the Lord Jesus who continually admonishes us by His Spirit to follow Him. If we are to live by His power and experience His sufficiency, we need to follow Him with all our hearts. So the way we live by the power of the Holy Spirit is *first* of all to recognize that *He is already at work in us creating in us both the will and power to do His good pleasure;* that, *He desires to lead us in an entirely new direction;* and that, *we must stay close to Him and obey His every command.*

But if the Spirit of Him who raised Jesus from the dead dwells in you, He who raised Christ from the dead will also give life to your mortal bodies by His Spirit who dwells in you. Therefore, brethren, we are debtors — not to the flesh, to live according to the flesh. For if you live according to the flesh you will die; but if by the Spirit you put to death the deeds of the body, you will live. For as many as are led by the Spirit of God, these are the sons of God (Romans 8:11-14).